The Secret of the Lord

A Biblical Understanding of God's Covenant Language

Richard W. Allen

The Secret of the Lord: A Biblical Understanding of God's Covenant Language (Basic Bible Series)

WHAT IS THE BASIC BIBLE SERIES

Welcome to the *Basic Bible Series*, a collection of essential guides designed to equip Christians with the foundational truths of our faith. The word "basic" implies that the series intends to cover the basics of Christianity that all believers should know about in their walk with God. It does not imply that the book has basic surface-level knowledge, it is far from that! Each book delves into a core element of Christianity, drawing directly from Scripture to illuminate its relevance for everyday life.

Whether you're just beginning your walk with Christ or have been journeying for years, these volumes provide clear, biblically grounded insights to strengthen your relationship with God and empower you to live out your faith authentically. My goal is to make the profound truths of the Bible accessible and the *Basic Bible Series* is an invitation to transformation. God doesn't want us merely informed; He longs for us to be conformed to the image of His Son. Let each book inspire you to go deeper in your faith. As you read, pray for wisdom to understand, discuss these truths with fellow believers, and apply them to your life. The fruits will follow. Thank you for joining me in the *Basic Bible Series*; may this volume on covenants enrich your walk with the Lord and draw you closer to His heart.

COVENANTS OF GOD

The *Covenants of God* collection of The *Basic Bible Series* is a comprehensive exploration of the sacred agreements that form the backbone of God's relationship with humanity, as revealed throughout Scripture. At its heart, the collection seeks to unveil the profound mystery of how God binds Himself to His creation through covenants, transforming abstract theological concepts into life-changing truths. These covenants represent God's unchanging faithfulness, His pursuit of intimacy with us, and His redemptive plan unfolding across generations. By delving into each major covenant, the series equips readers to move beyond surface-level faith, fostering a deeper reverence for God and a confident partnership with Him.

The first book in the series, *The Secret of the Lord*, lays the essential foundation by defining what a covenant truly is. It explores five core characteristics of a covenant, details the ten rituals of covenant-making, and uncovers three essential terms that reveal how God connects with us in covenant. Then the book teaches us how to unlock "the secret of the Lord" to receive the full blessings of the New Covenant that Jesus died on the cross for. Building on this definition, the series will dedicate subsequent books to the major covenants of the Bible, each one a standalone yet interconnected revelation of God's character and plan.

CONTENTS

THE SECRET IN ACTION

CHAPTER 1

UNDERSTANDING THE SECRET
OF THE LORD

Have you ever wondered why some Christians seem to carry a faith that lights up their lives? They pray with a steady confidence, as if they know their words reach a listening ear, trusting God's presence in every moment. Their joy often shines through, not just in easy times, but even amidst struggles, a quiet strength that holds them steady. They face challenges with a grace that feels almost unnatural, guided by a sense of purpose that ties all aspects of their lives together. They don't treat their faith as a chore. Rather, it's a living part of who they are.

On the other hand, there are Christians who show up faithfully, week after week, and pour effort into their spiritual lives. They might attend every service, read their Bible diligently, and pray with discipline, yet still feel a quiet ache inside. Their faith can feel more like a duty, a list of tasks to complete, than a source of life. Doubts might creep in, leaving them wondering if their prayers matter or if God has distanced Himself. They long for something deeper, watching others with a mix of hope and frustration, unsure why their dedication doesn't bring the sa me peace.

If this strikes a chord with you, take heart, you are not alone. Many believers have felt this disconnect at some point in their journey. The good news is that there is indeed a "secret" that can transform your walk with God, and it's not reserved for a select few. God longs to share it with you. He doesn't want it to be a secret. This secret lies in understanding His covenants, and it's a revelation promised to those who approach Him with reverence and awe. As we embark on this exploration together, we'll uncover how this divine mystery can shift your faith from tentative to triumphant, drawing you into a deeper, more intimate relationship with the Lord.

We find the foundation for this promise in Psalm 25:14, where David wrote,

"The secret of the Lord is with those who fear him, And He will show them His covenant."

The secret David was talking about is reserved for those who *"fear"* Him, and with that revelation comes an understanding of His covenant. But what does it mean to fear God, and how does this unlock the mysteries of His covenant?

FEARING GOD: WORSHIP, NOT TERROR

To unlock God's secret, we must first understand what it means to "fear" Him. In our modern context, the word fear often conjures images of dread or emotions tied to punishment or danger. But the biblical concept of fearing God is far richer and more beautiful. It's not about trembling in terror, it's about standing in awe of His goodness, power, and presence. To fear God is to worship Him with reverence, to honor Him above all else, and to live in a posture of deep respect for who He is.

Perhaps you've felt moments in your own life where approaching God feels heavy, maybe shadowed by worry about whether you're worthy or good enough or fear of what He might think of you. It's a struggle many face, one that can quietly distance us from His presence. But consider this: What might change if you approached God with awe instead of worry or unworthiness? Imagine lifting your eyes from your fears to His majesty, letting wonder at His love and power replace the weight of your struggles. This shift could transform how you pray, how you trust, and even how you rest in Him.

Jesus Himself illuminates this in Luke 4:8, during His temptation by the devil. When Satan offered Him the kingdoms of the world in exchange for worship, Jesus responded,

> *"For it is written, 'You shall worship the Lord your God, and Him only you shall serve.'"*

When Jesus said, *"For it is written,"* He was quoting Deuteronomy 6:13, which says,

> *"You shall fear the Lord your God and serve Him, and shall take oaths in His name."*

Notice the connection Jesus made: fearing God is synonymous with worshiping and serving Him alone. Where Deuteronomy uses the word "fear," the context of Jesus' temptation tied it to worship, showing us that this fear is not a cowering dread but a reverential devotion. It's an acknowledgment of God's majesty that flows from the heart into praise and obedience.

This reverential fear stands in stark contrast to the tormenting fear the enemy might stir in us—fear of circumstances, failure, or even God's judgment. Instead, it's a fear rooted in love and trust, a recognition of God's holiness that draws us closer rather than pushing us away. As we cultivate this posture of worshipful awe, God promises to reveal His secret: His covenant.

When we worship Him with all our heart, soul, and might, we position ourselves to receive insights into His covenant, His sacred way of relating to us. It's not about earning His favor through performance but about drawing near in awe, trusting that He desires to reveal Himself. As Proverbs 9:10 declares,

"The fear of the Lord is the beginning of wisdom,"

and this wisdom begins with grasping the covenant that binds us to Him. And it's in understanding this covenant that we find the key to the joy, confidence, and power we see in others and long for ourselves.

THE COVENANT: GOD'S SACRED BOND

So, what is this covenant that God promises to show us? At its core, a covenant is a binding agreement between two parties, often sealed with a solemn commitment that reflects the essence of their relationship. In today's world, marriage is the most commonly known expression of a covenant or perhaps a legal agreement two parties agree to. However, both of these are often broken through lawyers or loopholes in the contract.

But a biblical covenant that God enters into with man is far more profound. It's a sacred, unbreakable bond (at least on God's end), often sealed with blood, that unites them in a relationship of mutual commitment. In ancient times, covenants were solemn agreements where two parties became one, sharing assets, liabilities, and responsibilities. This is where the marriage analogy comes into play. A marriage covenant isn't just a promise; it's a complete merging of lives, a pledge that should endure beyond convenience or circumstance.

In the Bible, God establishes covenants with humanity as the framework for His interactions with us. The Bible itself is a book of covenants. The terms "Old Testament" and "New Testament" literally mean "Old Covenant" and "New Covenant." However, one of the greatest revelations in the whole Bible is that the New Covenant is not technically between us and God. It's between God the Father and God the Son. Jesus was our representative man, or covenant head, who stood on our behalf when He died on the cross.

We become part of the New Covenant by faith. It's not conditional on our ability to keep certain promises, on our holiness, on our conduct, or on our performance. It's based on our simple faith in Jesus and maintaining that faith in

Him. But it is conditional on the ability of Jesus to keep certain promises to God the Father. We know Jesus is going to keep His side of the covenant, and God will as well, which makes it unbreakable.

Understanding these covenants is foundational to grasping our relationship with God, because they reveal not just what God does, but why and how He does it. They set Christianity apart from other religions. While many faiths involve prayer, offerings, or moral codes, the concept of a personal, covenantal bond with the Creator is uniquely Judeo-Christian.

God, the Almighty, chooses to bind Himself to humanity through covenants. He doesn't deal with us capriciously or distantly. He enters into sacred agreements that reflect His unchanging character. And when we understand these covenants, we gain confidence and assurance in our faith.

Why? Because we realize God has staked His reputation on keeping His word. We live in a world where promises are broken daily—by politicians, businesses, even loved ones—but God stands apart. Numbers 23:19 declares,

"God is not a man, that He should lie, Nor a son of man, that He should repent. Has He said, and will He not do? Or has He spoken, and will He not make it good?"

God cannot lie, His nature is truth, and His covenants are sure.

A TAPESTRY OF COVENANTS

Throughout Scripture, God weaves a tapestry of covenants, each revealing more of His heart and plan. He made a covenant with creation, establishing order in the universe—day and night, seasons, and natural laws—binding Himself to sustain it (Genesis 8:22). In His covenant with Adam, God gave man dominion over the earth, setting terms of obedience in a relationship sealed by divine intent (Genesis 2:15-18). Marked by the rainbow, He covenanted with Noah, who acted as a covenant head for all mankind, vowing never again to destroy the earth with a flood (Genesis 9:12-17). With Abraham, He pledged descendants as numerous as the stars and a land for His people (Genesis 12:1-3; Genesis 15:18). Through Moses at Sinai, He established Israel as His chosen nation under the Law (Exodus 19:5-6). To David, He promised an everlasting kingdom, ultimately fulfilled in Jesus (2 Samuel 7:12-16). And in the New Covenant, sealed by Christ's blood, He offers forgiveness and eternal life to all who believe (Jeremiah 31:31-34; Hebrews 8:6).

These covenants build upon one another, culminating in the New Covenant through Jesus. Understanding them helps us see God's overarching plan and our place within it. They move us from being spectators of God's acts to participants in His ways as Psalms 103:7 notes:

> *"He made known his **ways** to Moses, His **acts** to the children of Israel."*

Moses knew the *why* and *how* behind God's actions because he grasped the covenant, while the Israelites only saw the *what*. When we understand covenant, we too can cooperate with God, aligning our lives with His purposes and know His ways like Moses.

STEPPING INTO THE SECRET

Many Christians today remain unaware of their significance. Without understanding covenant, we may see God's acts—His miracles, blessings, and judgments—but miss His ways, the deeper reasons behind His actions. This lack of understanding can leave us feeling distant from God, unsure of His promises or presence. As you learn to fear God, to worship Him with awe and reverence, He will reveal it to you.

In our culture riddled with broken promises and deception, it's easy to become cynical, even suspicious of God. Disappointment and doubt have become our conditioned responses. But He is not like us. He does not break His covenants with us, offering a foundation of trust in an unstable world. When we begin to see the Bible through the lens of covenant, our faith shifts from uncertainty to assurance, rooted in His unchanging word.

When you accept Christ, God promises to forgive your sins, write His laws on your heart, give you His Holy Spirit, and adopt you as His child (Jeremiah 31:33-34; Hebrews 8:10-12). This isn't based on your holiness or effort, it's anchored in Jesus' finished work on the cross. Understanding this covenant shifts your faith from uncertainty to certainty. You no longer question if God loves you or if His promises apply. You know that, because He's bound Himself to you, you're secure in His care.

You will not have assurance in the Kingdom of God and in your walk with God if you do not know the secret of the Lord. If His covenants are not revealed to you, you will be like the average Israelite wondering around the desert for 40 years. Some Christians go to church their whole lives, and though they may be saved, they do not know how God can truly bless their lives. Not because God doesn't want to reveal it, but because they just don't understand. You will not see the great things God's covenant can reveal to you if you do not fear God.

To understand how the secret of the Lord plays out in the real world, we need to look at ordinary individuals who embraced covenant with God and let it define their actions and destiny. In the next chapter, we'll turn to the lives of Moses, Elijah, Elisha, and David—men who didn't merely know about the secret of the Lord but lived it with extraordinary faith and courage. Their stories reveal how this divine insight turned them into powerful examples of God's presence and purpose, navigating challenges and triumphs with an unshakable trust in Him. More than historical accounts, these narratives invite us to explore how the secret to their lives can revitalize our own. Through these examples, you'll discover why others seem to walk in joy and power: they've tapped into the secret of the Lord. And that secret is yours to claim.

CHAPTER 2

COVENANT IN ACTION

The secret of the Lord is more than a concept, it's a dynamic force that reshapes lives. It's the key that unlocks a deeper connection with God, available to anyone willing to approach Him with reverence. But what does this look like when it's put to the test? How does this divine insight play out in the messiness of real life? To answer that, we turn to four men—Moses, Elijah, Elisha, and David—whose stories bring this secret into sharp focus.

These weren't superhumans or untouchable saints. They were flawed, relatable people who faced daunting challenges: a defiant Pharaoh refusing to free a nation, a hostile king and queen bent on idolatry, a menacing army encircling a lone prophet, and a towering giant defying God's people. Yet, their lives became extraordinary because they didn't just hear about God's covenant, they stepped into it. They trusted His promises, leaned on His presence, and let His purpose guide their every move. In this chapter, we'll dive into the defining moments that reveal how these men's grasp of the secret of the Lord fueled their courage and shaped their legacies. They show us that the secret of the Lord isn't a quiet theory, but a bold, active partnership with the Divine.

MOSES: INTERCEDING ON THE BASIS OF COVENANT

The story of Moses and the golden calf in Exodus 32 is a dramatic demonstration of covenant in action, a testament to the power of God's promises and the boldness of a man who stood on them. Moses, the reluctant leader who had guided the Israelites out of Egyptian slavery, found himself at a pivotal moment in their journey. Freshly liberated by God's mighty hand, the Israelites were encamped at the foot of Mount Sinai. Moses had ascended the mountain to receive the Ten Commandments, the foundational laws that would define their identity as God's chosen people. But below, the people grew restless.

Forty days had passed since Moses disappeared into the cloud-covered peak (Exodus 24:18). The Israelites, unaccustomed to such prolonged absence and still shaped by centuries of Egyptian idolatry, grew anxious. They approached Aaron, Moses' brother and deputy, demanding,

> *"Come, make us gods that shall go before us; for as for this Moses, the man who brought us up out of the land of Egypt, we do not know what has become of him."* (Exodus 32:1)

Aaron, perhaps overwhelmed or seeking to appease them, complied. He collected their gold earrings, melted them down, and fashioned a golden calf. The people proclaimed,

> *"This is your god, O Israel, that brought you out of the land of Egypt!"* (Exodus 32:4)

They offered sacrifices and indulged in revelry, blatantly violating the covenant they had just agreed to uphold (Exodus 19:8).

This act of idolatry was a direct affront to the God who had parted the Red Sea, rained manna from heaven, and spoke to them from the mountain. God's response was swift and severe. He interrupted Moses' communion on the mountaintop, declaring:

> *"Go, get down! For your people whom you brought out of the land of*
> *Egypt have corrupted themselves. They have turned aside quickly out*
> *of the way which I commanded them. They have made themselves a*
> *molded calf, and worshiped it and sacrificed to it, and said, 'This is*
> *your god, O Israel, that brought you out of the land of Egypt!' And*
> *the Lord said to Moses, 'I have seen this people, and indeed it is a*
> *stiff-necked people! Now therefore, let Me alone, that My wrath may*
> *burn hot against them and I may consume them. And I will make*
> *of you a great nation.'"* (Exodus 32:7-10)

Here was an astonishing proposition: God offered to start anew with Moses, wiping out the rebellious Israelites and building a new nation through him alone. For many, such an offer might have been tempting, a chance to escape the burden of leading a grumbling, disobedient people and to secure a legacy of honor. Yet Moses did not hesitate. Instead of accepting God's proposal, he interceded for the very people who had betrayed their Deliverer. His prayer was not a frantic plea driven by sentiment or desperation but a carefully reasoned appeal rooted in God's covenant:

> *"Lord, why does Your wrath burn hot against Your people whom*
> *You have brought out of the land of Egypt with great power and*
> *with a mighty hand? Why should the Egyptians speak, and say,*
> *'He brought them out to harm them, to kill them in the mountains,*
> *and to consume them from the face of the earth'? Turn from Your*
> *fierce wrath, and relent from this harm to Your people. Remember*
> *Abraham, Isaac, and Israel, Your servants, to whom You swore by*
> *Your own self, and said to them, 'I will multiply your descendants*
> *as the stars of heaven; and all this land that I have spoken of I*

give to your descendants, and they shall inherit it forever.'" (Exodus 32:11-13)

Moses' relationship with God set him apart and his intercession was striking for what it omitted. The Israelites had seen God's power from a distance, trembling at the thunder and fire on Sinai (Exodus 19:16-19). But Moses entered the cloud and communed with God. He did not defend the Israelites' actions, there was no defense to offer. Nor did he appeal to his own merits or emotions, which might have faltered under the weight of their sin. Instead, he anchored his plea in the covenant God had made with Abraham centuries earlier, a promise reaffirmed to Isaac and Jacob and sealed by God's own oath (Genesis 22:16-18). Moses understood the secret of the Lord, and his reverence and proximity to God revealed the covenant's depth, enabling him to intercede with authority. God's response was remarkable:

"So the Lord relented from the harm which He said He would do to His people." (Exodus 32:14)

This was not a capricious change of mind but a demonstration of God's responsiveness to covenant-based prayer. The Israelites were spared because Moses stood on the unshakable ground of God's promise.

But the drama was far from over. Descending with the tablets, Moses beheld the chaos below, the calf glinting in the sun and the people lost in frenzied worship. Rage and sorrow collided within him. With a cry, he cast the tablets down, their shattering a thunderous echo of the broken covenant (Exodus 32:19). Confronting Aaron's feeble excuses, he acted swiftly: he pulverized the idol, mixed its dust with water, and forced the people to drink the bitter consequence of their sin (Exodus 32:20). Yet even in judgment, his heart yearned for reconciliation. Returning to God with new tablets, he offered the ultimate sacrifice:

"Yet now, if You will forgive their sin—but if not, I pray, blot me
out of Your book which You have written." (Exodus 32:32)

Moses is essentially offering to sacrifice his own place in God's covenant, in exchange for God's forgiveness of the people's sin. God declined the trade but renewed the covenant, promising His presence (Exodus 34:10).

Moses' intercession reveals the power of covenant understanding. He didn't beg based on human merit (there was none) or sway God with emotion. He stood on the promise sworn to Abraham, trusting God's word over fleeting circumstances. Today, as heirs of the new covenant through Jesus' blood (Hebrews 8:6), we inherit this legacy. We can approach God boldly, not cringing in fear of rejection, but resting in His faithfulness. Whether praying for ourselves or interceding for others, we echo Moses, grounding our pleas in the eternal bond forged at the cross. In a world of broken promises, Moses shows us the strength of covenant ground, where God's word is our fortress, and His oath is our unshakable hope. Centuries later, Elijah would similarly stand on God's covenant promises, confronting a nation lost to idolatry with unwavering trust in the same faithful God.

ELIJAH: STANDING ON COVENANT PROMISES

The story of Elijah unfolds in 1 Kings 17 & 18, where Israel had fallen into a spiritual abyss under King Ahab and Queen Jezebel, a royal pair whose reign was a relentless assault on the covenant God had forged with His people. The land, once blessed with abundance, now bowed under the shadow of Baal, a Canaanite deity falsely heralded as the master of rain and fertility. Altars to the Lord crumbled into dust, overtaken by grotesque shrines where priests of Baal offered sacrifices amid swirling incense and frenzied chants. The people, seduced by Jezebel's fervor and Ahab's weakness, turned their backs on the God who had delivered them from Egypt, their idolatry a gaping wound in the covenant established at Sinai (Exodus

19:5-6). The air hung heavy with apostasy, and the earth itself seemed to groan under the weight of a nation unmoored.

Into this chaos emerged Elijah the Tishbite, a rugged figure whose very name, "The Lord is my God", was a defiant rebuke to the prevailing darkness. Clothed in a mantle of coarse hair, he carried no weapon but the word of God, his presence a living testament to the covenant's enduring power. Without summons or ceremony, Elijah stormed into Ahab's gilded palace, past guards who hesitated at his unflinching gaze, and stood before the king. The court fell silent, the clinking of goblets and murmurs of sycophants swallowed by the prophet's audacity. His voice rang out like a hammer on stone:

> *"As the Lord God of Israel lives, before whom I stand, there shall not be dew nor rain these years, except at my word."* (1 Kings 17:1)

No plea, no preamble, just a declaration that seized the heavens and shook the throne. Ahab, his face a mask of fury and fear, gripped the arms of his seat, but Elijah turned and vanished as swiftly as he had come, leaving the king to wrestle with a prophecy that brooked no compromise.

This was no reckless boast. Elijah's words were rooted in the covenant God had etched into Israel's soul through Moses. In Deuteronomy 28, the Lord had laid out the terms: obedience would bring blessings—rain, harvests, peace—while disobedience would unleash curses, including drought:

> *"The Lord will change the rain of your land to powder and dust; from the heaven it shall come down on you until you are destroyed."* (Deuteronomy 28:24)

Israel's worship of Baal had shattered their fidelity, and Elijah, a student of God's word, recognized the hour of judgment had struck. He wasn't acting on impulse or spite; he was enforcing the covenant's consequences, wielding its authority as a divine mandate. With his pronouncement, the skies locked shut, and the land began its slow descent into desolation.

For three and a half years, the drought gnawed at Israel's lifeblood. Rivers shrank to muddy threads, fields hardened into cracked wastelands, and the bleating of starving flocks faded into silence. The sun blazed mercilessly, turning the once-verdant hills into a graveyard of brittle thorns. Baal's priests cried out to their god, slashing themselves in desperate rituals, but the heavens mocked their pleas with unbroken silence. Famine tightened its grip, children's bellies swelled with hunger, and parents scavenged for scraps amid the dust. Ahab, clinging to his idols, sent scouts to hunt Elijah, blaming the prophet for a calamity born of his own sin.

God instructed Elijah to hide by the brook Cherith, east of the Jordan River. There, God commanded ravens to bring him bread and meat twice a day, morning and evening, while Elijah drank from the brook. Ravens, typically scavengers and unclean birds under Mosaic law (Leviticus 11:15), were an unusual choice for divine provision. Their role highlighted God's authority over nature, using even unlikely creatures to fulfill His purpose. The bread and meat met Elijah's basic needs in a desolate region where food was scarce due to the drought.

This provision lasted until the brook Cherith dried up, a consequence of the ongoing drought. The ravens' consistent delivery underscored God's faithfulness to His word, as He had promised to sustain Elijah. This act also reflected the covenant relationship: just as God provided manna and water for Israel in the wilderness (Exodus 16:4, 17:6), He ensured Elijah's survival, affirming His commitment to His servant and, by extension, His plan to call Israel back to covenant obedience.

When the brook Cherith dried up, God directed Elijah to Zarephath, a town in Sidon, a Gentile region under Jezebel's influence and thus hostile to Israel's God. God told Elijah that a widow there would provide for him. Upon arriving, Elijah found a widow gathering sticks, preparing to make a final meal for herself and her son with her last handful of flour and drop of oil, expecting to die of starvation afterward. Elijah asked her to make him a small cake first, assuring her,

"For thus says the Lord God of Israel: 'The bin of flour shall not be used up, nor shall the jar of oil run dry, until the day the Lord sends rain on the earth.'" (1 Kings 17:14)

The widow obeyed, and as promised, her flour bin and oil jar did not run out. She, her son, and Elijah were sustained for many days, likely months, until the drought ended. This miracle was localized to her household, as the broader region continued to suffer famine. The provision was modest, enough to make daily bread , but sufficient to preserve life. Later, when the widow's son died, Elijah prayed, and God restored the boy's life, further confirming God's power and presence through Elijah.

This event extended God's covenant faithfulness beyond Israel. The widow, a Gentile with no prior connection to Israel's God, experienced His provision by acting in faith. Her obedience mirrored the covenant principle of trusting God's promises, and her inclusion in the story foreshadowed God's ultimate plan to bless all nations through Abraham's seed (Genesis 22:18). For Elijah, the widow's provision ensured his survival, enabling him to continue his mission.

In the third year, as the nation teetered on collapse, the Lord spoke:

"Go, present yourself to Ahab, and I will send rain on the earth." (1 Kings 18:1)

The time for confrontation had arrived. Elijah emerged from hiding and met Ahab on a road choked with dust, the king's eyes hollow with rage.

"Is that you, O troubler of Israel?" (1 Kings 18:17)

Ahab spat. Elijah's response was unyielding:

"I have not troubled Israel, but you and your father's house have, in that you have forsaken the commandments of the Lord and have followed the Baals." (1 Kings 18:18)

He issued a challenge: gather the 450 prophets of Baal and the 400 prophets of Asherah to Mount Carmel for a showdown to determine the true God. Ahab, perhaps sensing a chance to crush the prophet, agreed, and the stage was set for a contest that would sear itself into Israel's memory.

Mount Carmel loomed over the parched landscape, its slopes a stark arena for the clash of powers. Two altars stood ready: one for Baal and one for the Lord. Elijah spoke,

"How long will you falter between two opinions? If the Lord is God, follow Him; but if Baal, follow him.' But the people answered him not a word." (1 Kings 18:21)

The terms were clear: each side would offer a bull cut into pieces, but no fire would be kindled by human hands. The God who answered with flame would prove His dominion. Baal's prophets took the lead, their voices rising in a cacophony of pleas:

"O Baal, hear us!" (1 Kings 18:26)

From morning to noon, they danced and shouted, their movements growing erratic as the hours bled away. They leapt upon their altar, knives flashing as they carved their flesh, blood dripping onto the stone in a grotesque appeal. Yet the sky remained a blank expanse, and Elijah's voice pierced their din:

"Cry aloud, for he is a god; either he is meditating, or he is busy, or he is on a journey, or perhaps he is sleeping and must be awakened." (1 Kings 18:27)

The taunt stung, but Baal's silence was deafening.

As the sun dipped toward afternoon, Elijah called the people closer. With deliberate care, he rebuilt the Lord's altar, gathering twelve stones, one for each tribe of Israel, a poignant echo of the covenant that bound them as one (Exodus 24:4). He arranged the wood, laid the sacrifice, and then, in a move that hushed the crowd, ordered four large jars of precious water to be poured over it all, three times over. Water soaked the offering, drenched the wood, and pooled in a trench he'd dug around the altar, an extravagant act in a land dying of thirst. The impossibility of fire seemed to mock human logic, yet Elijah stood serene, his faith unshaken. At the time of the evening sacrifice, he raised his voice in prayer:

"Lord God of Abraham, Isaac, and Israel, let it be known this day that You are God in Israel and I am Your servant, and that I have done all these things at Your word. Hear me, O Lord, hear me, that this people may know that You are the Lord God, and that You have turned their hearts back to You again." (1 Kings 18:36-37)

No theatrics, no shouting, just a plea grounded in covenant trust. The response was instantaneous. Fire fell from the heavens, a roaring column of divine fury that devoured the sacrifice, the wood, the stones, and even the water in the trench. God's presence was palpable in the mountain, ablaze in the fire's heat and light. The people staggered back, then fell to their faces, their voices erupting in awe:

"The Lord, He is God! The Lord, He is God!" (1 Kings 18:39)

In that moment, the chains of idolatry snapped, and repentance swept through the crowd like a wind. Elijah seized the momentum, commanding the people to seize Baal's prophets, who were led down to the Kishon Valley and executed, a stark fulfillment of the covenant's call to purge false worship (Deuteronomy 13:5).

But the land still thirsted. Elijah climbed higher on Carmel, bowing low with his face between his knees, and prayed for rain. Seven times he sent his servant to the cliff overlooking the sea, and seven times the horizon remained empty, until, at last, a cloud rose from the waters. Elijah leapt up, urgency in his voice:

> *"Go up, say to Ahab, 'Prepare your chariot, and go down before the rain stops you.'"* (1 Kings 18:44)

The sky darkened, winds howled, and there was a heavy rain, a deluge that drenched the earth and broke the drought's cruel grip. This was no coincidence; it was the covenant fulfilled, echoing Deuteronomy 28:12:

> *"The Lord will open to you His good treasure, the heavens, to give the rain to your land in its season, and to bless all the work of your hand."*

Elijah's intercession had unlocked the blessing tied to Israel's return to God.

Elijah's ministry reveals a man saturated in covenant knowledge and who knew the secret of the Lord. He knew when to invoke judgment, as with the drought, and when to plead for mercy, as with the rain, each step aligned with God's revealed will. His confidence sprang not from pride but from a deep grasp of Scripture, his every action a reflection of the covenant's terms. For us, Elijah's story is a call to immerse ourselves in God's word, to discern His promises, and to act with boldness, trusting that our authority rests not in ourselves but in knowing that God does not break His covenant with us. When we stand on His truth, as Elijah did, we can speak into the droughts of our lives—spiritual, emotional, or physical—and watch Him respond with fire and rain. This same covenant boldness marked the ministry of Elisha, Elijah's successor, who faced overwhelming danger with unshakable trust in God's protective promises.

ELISHA: CONFIDENCE IN COVENANT PROTECTION

Elisha, the prophet who succeeded Elijah, faced a moment of dire peril that tested the faith of those around him, as recorded in 2 Kings 6. The king of Syria, furious that Elisha's prophetic insight repeatedly foiled his military ambushes against Israel, resolved to eliminate the threat. He dispatched a formidable army to Dothan, where Elisha resided, surrounding the city under the cover of night.

At dawn, Elisha's servant rose and stepped outside, only to freeze in terror. The horizon was a wall of menace: a vast Syrian force encircled them. The servant's stomach dropped as he grasped their predicament. He stumbled back to Elisha, gasping,

"Alas, my master! What shall we do?" (2 Kings 6:15)

Every sound, the clank of armor, the creak of chariot wheels, amplified his dread, painting a picture of inescapable doom.

Yet Elisha remained a pillar of calm amid the storm. His eyes, steady and unshaken, met the servant's wild, fearful stare.

"Do not fear, for those who are with us are more than those who are with them." (2 Kings 6:16)

The servant blinked, incredulous, peering again at the encircling horde. To him, Elisha's words seemed like madness, how could two men outmatch thousands? But Elisha's confidence was not rooted in human logic; it flowed from his deep trust in God's covenant promise of protection. Lifting his hands, he prayed with quiet authority:

"Lord, I pray, open his eyes that he may see." (2 Kings 6:17)

God opened the servant's eyes to reveal His angelic host,

"the mountain was full of horses and chariots of fire all around Elisha." (2 Kings 6:17)

In that moment, the servant's world transformed. The hills around Dothan, moments ago filled with dread of the enemy, erupted into blinding splendor. A heavenly army materialized, countless angelic warriors, their forms radiant with divine fire, stood poised on the mountainside. Their numbers dwarfed the Syrian forces, stretching across the ridges in a host too vast to count, their presence a roaring testament to God's might. These were the guardians of God's covenant, sent to shield His prophet, invisible until now but ever-present. The Syrian army, once an overwhelming terror, now seemed a frail shadow against this divine host.

Elisha's faith was anchored in the covenant God forged with Israel at Sinai. He knew the promise of Psalm 91:11-12:

"For He shall give His angels charge over you, To keep you in all your ways. In their hands they shall bear you up, Lest you dash your foot against a stone."

This was a binding pledge of divine defense for those who honored God. Elisha understood that no earthly force could sever this shield of faithfulness. With this assurance, he acted boldly. He prayed again and God answered,

"Strike this people, I pray, with blindness" (2 Kings 6:18),

and God did so.

Then, in an amazing turn of events, Elisha, the one they were searching for, convinced the blinded army to follow him to Samaria, a city deep within Israelite territory. This was a terrible move for the Syrians because it was the capital of Israel, the very heart of their enemy's land. By following Elisha there, the Syrians were stumbling blindly into a stronghold where Israelite soldiers and defenses surrounded them. They were far from home, with no allies nearby, walking straight into a situation where they were completely vulnerable, like sheep wandering into a lion's den. So not only were they supernaturally blind, but supernaturally dumb, totally unaware of the danger they were stepping i nto!

Once they got there, the army's sight was restored. That must have been a rude awakening to be in the middle of the enemy's camp. The king of Israel asked Elisha if they should kill the entire army. Rather than slaughter them, he instructed the king of Israel to feed them and give them drink so as to avoid war.

> *"You shall not kill them. Would you kill those whom you have taken captive with your sword and your bow? Set food and water before them, that they may eat and drink and go to their master."* (2 Kings 6:22)

This act of mercy led to peace:

> *"So the bands of Syrian raiders came no more into the land of Israel."* (2 Kings 6:23)

Elisha's strategy reflected Deuteronomy 28:28 (which was written approximately 550 years earlier), where God promised to strike Israel's enemies with,

> *"madness and blindness and confusion of heart,"*

for disobedience. His mercy also reflects Proverbs 25:21-22, which is also cited in Romans 12:20,

> *"If your enemy is hungry, give him bread to eat; And if he is thirsty, give him water to drink; For so you will heap coals of fire on his head, And the Lord will reward you."*

Proverbs and Romans were written 100 years and 850 years respectively after Elisha's story, showing the lasting effect of the covenant of Sinai.

At first glance, there seems to be some contradictory terms of giving your enemy food and water and *"heaping coals of fire"* on their head. This sounds like an act of harm or vengeance. However, a closer look at the historical and cultural context reveals a much different, and more profound meaning. In ancient Near Eastern culture, fire was a vital resource for survival used for cooking, warmth, and light. People often transported fire by carrying hot coals in a container, typically balanced on the head, from one place to another. Sharing coals was an act of generosity, providing someone with the means to sustain life. This practice gives the phrase, *"heap coals of fire upon his head,"* a positive connotation. It symbolizes giving something valuable and essential to another person.

Elisha didn't get a word from God to do all this. He was standing on the covenant where God had said to bless their enemies, and God would bless them back. His understanding of covenant and the secret of the Lord transformed a military threat into a diplomatic victory. For us, Elisha's example shows that covenant understanding brings peace in chaos. When we trust God's promise to protect, like,

> *"I am your shield,"* (Genesis 15:1)

we can face overwhelming odds with serenity, knowing His unseen forces are at work. This same covenant trust empowered David, who, like Elisha, faced an impossible foe by relying on God's enduring promise of victory for His people.

DAVID: COVENANT FAITH OVERCOMES GIANTS

David's triumph over Goliath in 1 Samuel 17 stands as one of the most celebrated demonstrations of covenant faith in Scripture. For forty days, the armies of Israel and the Philistines faced each other in a tense standoff across the Valley of Elah, a narrow stretch of land nestled in the foothills of Judah. The Philistines, a warlike people who had migrated from the Aegean region and settled along the coastal plains of Canaan, were perennial adversaries of Israel. Their frequent incursions into Israelite territory had long threatened the sovereignty of God's chosen people. This time, they proposed a battle of champions, a practice rooted in ancient Near Eastern warfare, where each side selected a single warrior to fight on behalf of the entire army. The outcome would decide the fate of both nations: if Goliath prevailed, Israel would become slaves to the Philistines; if an Israelite defeated him, the Philistines would serve Israel.

The Philistines' champion was Goliath of Gath, a towering figure whose physical presence alone was enough to paralyze Israel's forces with fear. Standing over nine feet tall, Goliath was a giant even among his own people. His bronze armor, weighing 125 pounds, gleamed in the sunlight, and his massive spear—its shaft as thick as a weaver's beam and tipped with a heavy iron head—promised death to any opponent. Each day, morning and evening, Goliath marched into the valley with his shield-bearer ahead of him, his deep voice thundering across the battlefield:

> *"I defy the armies of Israel this day; give me a man, that we may fight together!"* (1 Samuel 17:10)

For forty days, his taunts went unanswered. King Saul, once a formidable warrior, now sat in his tent, his courage eroded by the giant's relentless challenges and the weight of his own faltering leadership.

Into this scene of despair stepped David, a young shepherd from Bethlehem. He had been sent by his father, Jesse, to bring food to his older brothers, who were serving in Saul's army. David was no soldier; he was likely in his mid-teens, with ruddy cheeks and hands more accustomed to a shepherd's staff than a sword. Yet David was a boy who feared God, and through that reverence, the secret of the Lord had been revealed to him. As he approached the Israelite camp, Goliath's latest defiance echoed through the valley. While Saul's men shrank back, whispering among themselves in terror, David's response was one of righteous indignation:

> *"Who is this uncircumcised Philistine, that he should defy the armies of the living God?"* (1 Samuel 17:26)

To David, this was not a military threat but a spiritual outrage, an attack on the honor of God and His covenant people.

The heart of David's indignation lay in his understanding of the covenant that bound Israel to God. Circumcision, established in Genesis 17:10-14, was the physical sign of this covenant, first given to Abraham as a mark of God's promise. Through this covenant, God had pledged to make Abraham's descendants a great nation, to bless them, and to give them the land of Canaan as an everlasting possession (Genesis 17:7-8). Circumcision was more than a ritual; it was a visible declaration that Israel belonged to God in a way that set them apart from all other nations. Goliath, as an *"uncircumcised Philistine,"* stood outside this sacred bond. In David's eyes, the giant had no right to challenge the *"armies of the living God,"* for Israel's strength came not from their numbers or weapons, but from their covenant relationship with the Almighty.

David's faith was not abstract; it was forged through experience. As a shepherd, he had faced predators, such as lions and bears, that threatened his flock. In those moments, God had delivered him, proving His faithfulness to His promises. David told Saul,

"The Lord, who delivered me from the paw of the lion and from the paw of the bear, He will deliver me from the hand of this Philistine." (1 Samuel 17:37)

This was not bravado; it was a conviction rooted in God's past acts of deliverance, which David saw as guarantees of future victory.

Saul's reaction to David's boldness was one of skepticism.

"You are not able to go against this Philistine to fight with him; for you are a youth, and he a man of war from his youth." (1 Samuel 17:33)

Yet, with no other volunteers and the situation growing desperate, Saul relented. He offered David his own royal armor, perhaps hoping to bolster the boy's chances. But the armor, crafted for a seasoned king, hung awkwardly on David's slight frame. After a few steps, he shed it, choosing instead the tools he knew best: a sling, a staff, and five smooth stones plucked from the brook that ran through the Valley of Elah. David was not relying on human equipment; he was staking everything on the God who had promised to fight for Israel, as He had declared to M oses:

"The Lord will fight for you, and you shall hold your peace." (Exodus 14:14)

When David descended into the valley to face Goliath, the giant's contempt was palpable. Goliath sneered as he eyed David's shepherd's staff,

"Am I a dog, that you come to me with sticks?" (1 Samuel 17:43)

Cursing David by his pagan gods, Goliath roared,

"Come to me, and I will give your flesh to the birds of the air and the beasts of the field!" (1 Samuel 17:44)

Undaunted, David met the giant's threats with a proclamation of faith:

"You come to me with a sword, with a spear, and with a javelin. But I come to you in the name of the Lord of hosts, the God of the armies of Israel, whom you have defied. This day the Lord will deliver you into my hand, and I will strike you and take your head from you...that all the earth may know that there is a God in Israel." (1 Samuel 17:45-46)

With those words, David charged forward. He placed a stone in his sling, swung it with practiced precision, and released. The stone flew true, striking Goliath in the forehead. The giant's massive form crumpled, his face hitting the dust as the armies on both sides held their breath. David ran to the fallen warrior, drew Goliath's own sword from its sheath, and severed his head, sealing Israel's victory. The Philistines, stunned and leaderless, turned and fled, pursued by the emboldened Israelites.

David's triumph was not a testament to his skill, though his years as a shepherd had honed his aim, but to his trust in God's covenant promises. He knew the secret of the Lord, His steadfast commitment to His people. As a representative of Israel, David acted as a covenant head; his faith and victory were credited to the entire nation. This foreshadows the greater victory of Jesus Christ, the ultimate Son of David, whose faithfulness as the covenant head secures salvation for all who trust in Him.

THE COMMON THREAD

What unites Moses, Elijah, Elisha, and David? Each feared God, worshiping Him with reverence, and understood His covenant. Psalm 25:14 promises that God reveals His secrets to such people, and these men lived it out. Moses interceded boldly, Elijah enforced covenant terms, Elisha trusted divine protection, and David vanquished a giant, all because they grasped God's sacred bond. They weren't superhuman; they were transformed by their relationship with God. This intimacy empowered them to partner with God, shifting history through their actions.

Their lives counter the average Israelite, or Christian, who drifts through life wondering why God moves for others but not them. The difference isn't divine favoritism, it's covenant awareness. These men stood head and shoulders above the pack, not by destiny alone, but by choice, to worship God and embrace His covenant. By fearing God and seeking to understand His covenant, you too can step into the joy, confidence, and authority that comes from knowing you are bound to Him in an unbreakable union.

To truly unlock this revelation, you must first understand what a covenant is: a blood bond broken only by death, sealed with a sacred oath, marked by unending loyalty and faithfulness, and forging a complete union of two parties. You need to grasp how a covenant is cut—through the shedding of blood, the mingling of lives, and the solemn oaths that bind the parties together. The rituals behind covenant are profound acts that embody loyalty, identity, and mutual responsibility—like the cutting of flesh and creating a permanent scar, a representative covenant head acting on behalf of others, exchanging names, belts, and garments, cutting animals in half, and sealing the covenant with terms, a lasting monument, and a shared meal. And you must become familiar with covenant terminology—words like "friend," "remember," and "lovingkindness," which carry deep covenantal weight in Scripture, pointing to the nature of God's relationship with us. Only with this foundation and committing to worshiping Him deeply can you fully comprehend the covenants God has made with His people from Adam to Christ. In doing so, He unfolds the secrets of His heart, showing you the depth of His love and commitment through His covenants.

FIVE ELEMENTS OF A COVENANT

There are five defining characteristics of a covenant that are essential to study if the secret of the Lord is to be revealed to you. In the next chapter each element is discussed individually. Then all five elements are tied together in the marriage covenant to make them personally relatable to Christians today.

A covenant has the following elements:

1 – **IS A BLOOD BOND**
2 – **IS AN UNBREAKABLE AGREEMENT**
3 – **HAS A SACRED OATH**
4 – **EMBODIES LOYALTY & FAITHFULNESS**
5 – **UNITES TWO PARTIES**

CHAPTER 3

DEFINING COVENANT

In the previous chapters, we explored the secret of the Lord as revealed to those who fear Him—a secret intricately tied to His covenant—and witnessed its transformative power in the lives of figures like Moses, Elijah, Elisha, and David. These men, through their reverential worship of God and their understanding of His covenant, lived with extraordinary confidence and partnered with Him in His divine purposes.

Now, we turn our attention to unpacking the very essence of this concept. What is a covenant? The word covenant is found throughout Scripture, yet for many believers today, its meaning remains shrouded in mystery or reduced to a vague notion of agreement. To truly grasp its significance, we must dig into its biblical roots and cultural implications. God conceived the idea of covenant, and it is through covenants that He operates in the earth. Most Christians don't realize how important covenants are to their lives and walks with God. Covenant touches the essence of life and that's why it's such a powerful word.

In the pages that follow, we will walk through five defining characteristics of a covenant: its nature as a blood bond, an unbreakable agreement, a sacred oath, a pledge of unending loyalty and faithfulness, and a unifying force that binds two parties into one. These characteristics illuminate the depth and power of God's covenantal relationship with us. To bring this concept closer to home, we will then explore how these traits manifest in the marriage covenant, a sacred bond that most people, whether believers or non-believers, can relate to. By examining marriage through the lens of these covenantal principles, we will see how God's design for human relationships mirrors His eternal commitment to His people, offering a tangible reflection of His divine faithfulness.

A COVENANT IS A BLOOD BOND

The Hebrew word for covenant is *berith*, a term that literally means "to cut till bleeding occurs." This vivid definition unveils the gravity and depth of what a covenant entails. In biblical times, people often sealed covenants with blood, a symbol of life itself, underscoring their permanence and the life-and-death commitment they demanded. As Leviticus 17:11 declares,

"For the life of the flesh is in the blood."

Blood represents life and was central to these sacred bonds. It represented the essence of existence, binding parties together in a way that transcended casual promises. When parties entered a covenant, they often mingled their blood, whether through cutting their flesh or sacrificing an animal, symbolizing that their lives were now intertwined. By incorporating blood into a covenant, the parties demonstrated their willingness to offer something vital. This act showed that the covenant was a matter of utmost importance, with consequences as severe as death for breaking it. The act of shedding or mixing blood symbolized the merging of identities.

There are many examples in the Bible where covenants are depicted as solemn agreements between God and humans, with blood frequently serving as a symbol or seal of their binding nature. In Genesis 15, God confirmed His promises to Abraham—descendants, land, and blessings—through a blood covenant ritual. Abraham was instructed to sacrifice specific animals and cut them in half, laying the pieces opposite each other. God then passed between the pieces as a smoking firepot and blazing torch, symbolizing His commitment. This act, known as a self-maledictory oath, meant that breaking the covenant would result in consequences akin to the fate of the sacrificed animals. God is not capable of breaking His covenants, so the consequences fall on man if they break the covenant.

In Genesis 17, God instituted circumcision as a physical sign of the covenant with Abraham, involving the shedding of blood. This ritual marked Abraham's male descendants, symbolizing their separation and dedication to God. It was a perpetual reminder of the covenant, extending to future generations and emphasizing the blood bond's continuity.

In Exodus 24:8, after reading the Ten Commandments to the Israelites, Moses sacrificed animals and sprinkled their blood on the people, declaring,

"This is the blood of the covenant that the Lord has made with you."

This act explicitly tied the covenant to blood, sealing the agreement between God and the Israelites and highlighted its sacred and binding nature.

In Luke 22:20, during the Last Supper, Jesus declared,

"This cup is the new covenant in my blood, which is shed for you."

With this, Jesus established the new covenant through His sacrificial death. His blood, shed on the cross, fulfilled and renewed God's relationship with humanity, offering forgiveness of sins and the empowering presence of the Holy Spirit. Hebrews 9:22 (NIV) emphasizes that,

"Without the shedding of blood there is no forgiveness."

This highlights the necessity of Christ's death to ratify the new covenant. This new covenant extends to all who trust in Jesus, transcending the limitations of the Mosaic covenant.

Blood covenants were not unique to the Bible but were common in ancient Near Eastern cultures, such as among the Hittites and tribal groups in Africa and the Middle East, where blood was mingled to show a bond. However, biblical blood covenants are distinct in that God instituted them, provided the terms, and took personal responsibility for fulfillment.

A COVENANT IS AN UNBREAKABLE AGREEMENT

A covenant is a solemn, binding commitment between two or more parties, often characterized as an unbreakable agreement when God is the one who enters the covenant. God will not break His commitment to man in covenant although man in our imperfect state is prone to breaking our side of the covenant. Unlike a casual promise or a contract that can be renegotiated, a covenant carries a profound sense of permanence and obligation. Its nature stems from deep trust, mutual responsibilities, and often a higher moral or spiritual authority that underpins it. The term "unbreakable" refers to covenants that are unconditional, meaning God will fulfill them regardless of human obedience or disobedience. These are contrasted with conditional covenants, like the Mosaic Covenant, which depend on human adherence to terms.

Covenants are designed to last, sometimes for a lifetime or across generations. Covenants are not easily dissolved. The first example of an unbreakable covenant is seen in Genesis. After the flood, God established a covenant with Noah and all living creatures, promising never to destroy the earth with water again. Genesis 9:16 states,

> *"The rainbow shall be in the cloud, and I will look on it to remember the everlasting covenant between God and every living creature of all flesh that is on the earth."*

This covenant is unconditional, depending solely on God's promise, and its sign, the rainbow, serves as a perpetual reminder. The fact that there has not been another global flood is seen as evidence of its unbreakability, illustrating God's faithfulness to all creation.

In the Abrahamic covenant, God promised Abraham that he would be the father of a great nation, that his descendants would inherit the land of Canaan, and that through him all nations would be blessed. This covenant is explicitly called *"everlasting"* in Genesis 17:7, 13, and 19, stating,

> *"I will establish My covenant between Me and you and your descendants after you in their generations, for an everlasting covenant, to be God to you and your descendants after you."*

Despite human errors, such as Abraham's doubt when he laughed at the promise of a son in his old age, questioning how he and Sarah could bear a child (Genesis 17:17), and Sarah's attempt to fulfill the promise through her servant Hagar, resulting in the birth of Ishmael (Genesis 16:1-4), God remained steadfast.

Abraham's skepticism stemmed from his advanced age, nearing 100, and Sarah's barrenness, leading him to propose that Ishmael, born to Hagar, might be the heir (Genesis 17:18). Sarah, impatient and doubting her own ability to conceive, urged Abraham to take Hagar as a surrogate, hoping to build a family through her, a common practice in their culture but a deviation from God's plan. These actions reflect their struggle to trust God's timing, yet God reaffirmed the promise in Isaac, the child of Sarah, born miraculously in their old age (Genesis 21:1-3), and extended it to Isaac (Genesis 26:3-5) and Jacob (Genesis 28:13-15), showing the covenant's unbreakability. Galatians 3:16-18 further interprets this as fulfilled through Christ, the ultimate seed of Abraham, emphasizing its enduring nature across generations and its universal blessing.

In the Davidic covenant, God promised David that his house, kingdom, and throne would be established forever. This covenant is unconditional, as seen in Psalm 89:34, where God declares,

"My covenant I will not break, nor alter the word that has gone out of My lips."

Despite the sins of David's descendants, like Solomon's idolatry, God preserved the line, leading to Jesus, the eternal King, fulfilling this promise. This illustrates its unbreakability, rooted in God's sovereign plan.

Prophesied in the Old Testament, the New Covenant promises forgiveness of sins, the indwelling of the Holy Spirit, and a direct relationship with God, written on the hearts of His people. Jeremiah 31:31-33 (NIV) states,

> *"The days are coming, declares the Lord, when I will make a new covenant with the people of Israel and with the people of Judah. It will not be like the covenant I made with their ancestors... because they broke my covenant...But this is the covenant I will make...I will put my law in their minds and write it on their hearts."*

It was fulfilled through Jesus, as seen in Luke 22:20,

> *"This cup is the new covenant in my blood,"*

and Hebrews 8:6-13, which quotes Jeremiah and calls it *"better"* and *"established on better promises."* Its unbreakability is evident in its basis on God's grace, not human effort, ensuring its permanence for all who trust in Christ.

Unbreakable covenants reflect God's character as faithful and unchanging, contrasting with human covenants that can be broken. In ancient Near Eastern cultures, covenants often involved self-maledictory oaths, where breaking the covenant invoked consequences, but biblical covenants, especially unconditional ones, emphasize God's initiative and reliability.

A COVENANT HAS A SACRED OATH

Central to the establishment of many covenants is the sacred oath—a solemn promise, often invoking God as a witness, to ensure the seriousness and binding nature of the agreement. Sacred oaths in the Bible were given in various ways, reflecting the cultural practices of the time and the gravity of the commitments being made. Through verbal declarations, symbolic actions, tangible signs, and the invocation of God's name, these oaths underscored the life-and-death consequences of covenant fidelity.

A good example of a sacred oath occurs in Genesis 21 where Abraham makes a covenant with Abimelech, a Philistine king, regarding the well at Beersheba. In this human-to-human agreement, both parties swear an oath to ensure peaceful relations and mutual respect. Abraham gives Abimelech seven ewe lambs as a tangible sign of the covenant, saying,

> "'You will take these seven ewe lambs from my hand, that they may be my witness that I have dug this well.' Therefore he called that place Beersheba, because the two of them swore an oath there. Thus they made a covenant at Beersheba." (Genesis 21:30-32)

The verbal oath, combined with the giving of animals, serves as a binding witness to their agreement. The place is named Beersheba, meaning "well of the oath," forever memorializing the sacred promise exchanged between the two men. This example illustrates how oaths in interpersonal covenants were reinforced by both spoken words and physical tokens, ensuring accountability.

Another notable instance of a sacred oath in covenant making is found in 2 Chronicles 15:11-15, during King Asa's reign:

> "They offered to the Lord at that time seven hundred bulls and seven thousand sheep from the spoil they had brought. Then they entered into a covenant to seek the Lord God of their fathers with all their

*heart and with all their soul; and whoever would not seek the Lord
God of Israel was to be put to death, whether small or great, whether
man or woman. Then they took an oath before the Lord with a loud
voice, with shouting and trumpets and rams' horns. And all Judah
rejoiced at the oath, for they had sworn with all their heart and
sought Him with all their soul; and He was found by them, and the
Lord gave them rest all around."*

King Asa inherited a kingdom steeped in idolatry from his father and grandfather but he pursued bold reforms, removing pagan altars, idols and even his
grandmother for her Asherah worship, ushering in a decade of peace (2 Chronicles 14:3–5; 15:16). Inspired by the prophet Azariah, Asa led the people of Judah
to enter a covenant to seek the Lord with all their hearts and souls. This was
meant to deepen their commitment to the Lord, warning against complacency
and promising God's presence if they sought Him (2 Chronicles 15:1–7).

Motivated by this prophetic call, Asa lead a national covenant sealed with
sacrifices and a sacred oath, invoking God to demonstrate their earnest commitment to this spiritual reform. This collective oath underscored the gravity of
their promise to abandon idolatry and return to true worship, and the people
rejoiced in their renewed dedication to God. This example highlights how sacred
oaths could drive national spiritual renewal, binding the community to a shared
commitment of faithfulness.

Sacred oaths in biblical covenant making were multifaceted, involving spoken
promises, ritual actions, physical tokens, and divine invocation. These elements
worked together to create a binding agreement that was not only legally en-
forceable but also spiritually significant. Whether between God and humanity
or among humans, these oaths reflected the deep relational and moral commitments that shaped the biblical narrative. Through these sacred promises, the Bible
portrays a world where words, actions, and divine witness intertwine to establish
relationships of trust, fidelity, and accountability.

A COVENANT EMBODIES LOYALTY & FAITHFULNESS

God's unwavering covenantal loyalty stands as a steadfast anchor in a world where faithfulness is often conditional and abandoned when inconvenient. We have to know that God is loyal and faithful and that we can count on Him. God does not break covenant. He cannot and will not break His word. When God says something, He keeps His promise. He will not lie to you. He will not leave you. He will not forsake you. He will not fail you. He will not let you go. He will not let you down. Do you know anybody in this life that would do the same for you? Lamentations 3:22-23 proclaims,

> *"Through the Lord's mercies we are not consumed, Because His compassions fail not. They are new every morning; Great is Your faithfulness."*

God's merciful nature renews His relationship with His people daily, effectively forgiving their sins and offering a fresh start every morning. Even when Israel strayed, God's commitment held fast, not because of their merit, but because of His covenantal nature of being a loyal and faithful God.

A covenant is, by its nature, a long-term commitment, often lasting a lifetime or spanning generations. It is not a temporary arrangement but a pledge meant to withstand the test of time. The notion of unending loyalty and faithfulness is woven into their very fabric, often expressed through terms like "everlasting" and "forever," signaling their eternal nature. Loyalty and faithfulness are essential to upholding this enduring bond for several reasons. Loyalty fosters trust, which is the bedrock of any covenant. When parties remain faithful, they create a secure environment where the relationship can thrive. This trust ensures that each side can rely on the other to fulfill their promises, even in difficult circumstances. A covenant often unites individuals or groups under a common goal or identity. Loyalty binds them together, ensuring that they remain aligned in their mission or relationship.

Faithfulness reinforces this unity, as it requires consistent action toward the covenant's purpose. Life's challenges—whether personal, social, or spiritual—can strain any relationship. Unending loyalty and faithfulness provide the strength to navigate these trials without abandoning the covenant. They act as a safeguard, ensuring that the bond remains intact even when tested. Loyalty and faithfulness reflect a moral commitment to honor the covenant, not just out of obligation but out of reverence for its deeper significance. These elements make loyalty and faithfulness indispensable to a covenant's integrity. Without them, the covenant risks becoming a hollow promise, easily broken when convenience or self-interest takes precedence.

Let's look at the Noahic Covenant in Genesis 9 again but under the guise of unending loyalty and faithfulness. The covenant's unconditional nature, no stipulations are placed on humanity, further illustrates God's unwavering loyalty. Despite the potential for human sin to persist, as it did before the flood, God committed to preserving life, extending His faithfulness to all creation in an enduring act of grace.

In the Davidic Covenant, God told David that his,

"kingdom shall be established forever." (2 Samuel 7:16)

This divine pledge revealed His unyielding commitment to an eternal purpose. The word *"forever"* underscores the unending nature of this promise, a pledge fulfilled in Jesus, the *"Son of David,"* whose eternal reign brings to life the Messianic hope. Even as Israel's monarchy crumbled through turmoil and exile, God's faithfulness to David's line stood unshaken, proving His steadfast loyalty across the sweeping arc of history.

The New Covenant embodies the pinnacle of God's unwavering loyalty and faithfulness, brought to life through Jesus Christ. To bridge Old Testament prophecy in Jeremiah 31 with New Testament fulfillment, God promised,

> *"This is the covenant that I will make with them...Their sins and their lawless deeds I will remember no more."* (Hebrews 10:16-17)

This pledge of complete forgiveness ushers in an eternal relationship with Him. Sealed by Christ's sacrificial blood, as He declared in Matthew 26:28,

> *"This is My blood of the new covenant, which is shed for many for the remission of sins."*

This everlasting covenant surpasses all prior agreements in its intimacy and scope. Unlike the Sinaitic Covenant between God and the Israelites which was rooted in external obedience, this one forges a direct, personal bond with God, open to all who believe. Through Jesus' death and resurrection, God's relentless commitment to redeem humanity shines forth, offering a faithfulness that stretches into eternity.

These covenants collectively embody unending loyalty and faithfulness in several distinct ways. First, their language—replete with terms like "everlasting" and "forever"—signals a divine intent for permanence, far beyond temporary human agreements. This eternal quality assures that God's promises are not subject to revocation or decay. Second, the unconditional nature of many covenants highlights God's reliability. His loyalty persists regardless of human shortcomings, a stark contrast to conditional human relationships. Third, the progressive fulfillment of these covenants through Jesus Christ ties them together across time, revealing a cohesive plan of faithfulness. From the rainbow's assurance to the cross's redemption, God's word remains unbroken, spanning millennia.

In essence, biblical covenants embody unending loyalty and faithfulness by serving as conduits of God's eternal promises, sustained by His unchanging nature. They offer humanity not just a series of divine pledges but a living relationship with a God who keeps His word across all time. Whether through the rainbow, the stars, the throne, or the cross, these covenants testify to a faithfulness that endures forever, inviting trust and hope in the One who never fails.

A COVENANT UNITES TWO PARTIES

Covenants are sacred agreements that bring two parties together, creating a unified relationship through shared promises and commitments. The concept of a covenant in Hebrew implies a deep, kinship-like bond, where the parties are united in purpose, identity, and loyalty. There are various ways covenants in the Bible unite two parties which can be between God and humanity or between humans, fostering a sense of connection and mutual obligation. Unity is at the heart of a covenant, as it transforms the parties into a cohesive entity with a shared destiny.

In the sacred covenant between God and Israel, God declared to His chosen people,

> *"If you will indeed obey My voice and keep My covenant, then you shall be a special treasure to Me above all people... a kingdom of priests and a holy nation."* (Exodus 19:5-6)

This divine agreement intertwined Israel's identity with God's guidance and blessings. God pledged to be their God, offering protection, provision, and purpose, while they committed to follow His laws. Yet, in God's covenant with us through Christ, this union deepens profoundly. As Paul wrote,

> *"God made him who had no sin to be sin for us, so that in him we might become the righteousness of God."* (2 Corinthians 5:21, NIV)

Through Christ, we inherit His righteousness, while He bears our sin. His strength and grace become ours, and His sufficiency covers our weaknesses, forging an intimate bond that surpasses even the covenant with Israel.

Human to human covenants in the Bible also illustrate how these agreements unite parties, often through personal bonds of loyalty and trust. The covenant between David and Jonathan, forged in the crucible of loyalty and trust, vividly illustrates how human-human covenants in the Bible unite individuals through deep personal bonds. As 1 Samuel 18:1-3 (NIV) recounts,

> *"Jonathan became one in spirit with David, and he loved him as himself... And Jonathan made a covenant with David because he loved him as himself."*

Despite Jonathan's position as the son of King Saul, who relentlessly pursued David's life, their friendship transcended political strife. In 1 Samuel 20:16-17 (NIV), Jonathan solidified this bond, declaring,

> *"So Jonathan made a covenant with the house of David, saying, 'May the Lord call David's enemies to account.' And Jonathan had David reaffirm his oath out of love for him, because he loved him as he loved himself."*

Jonathan vowed to shield David from harm, while David promised to care for Jonathan's descendants. This covenant wove their lives together, creating a profound connection that withstood external dangers and conflicting allegiances, showcasing how such agreements can forge enduring unity through mutual devotion.

Through all biblical covenants, whether between God and humanity or among humans, the unifying power of these sacred agreements shines as a testament to the enduring nature of relational bonds. These covenants reveal a profound truth: unity is not just a byproduct but the very essence of a covenant, weaving two parties into a cohesive whole, bound by trust, commitment, and a shared destiny.

DEFINING COVENANT THROUGH MARRIAGE

Among human relationships, marriage stands as the most intimate and powerful reflection of a covenant relationship. It is not by accident that the Bible frequently uses marriage as a metaphor for God's relationship with His people. Just as God enters an unbreakable covenant with humanity, so too do a man and a woman enter into a lifelong covenant with each other in marriage.

MARRIAGE AS A BLOOD BOND

In the context of marriage, the blood bond takes on both a symbolic and, in some traditions, a literal significance. The act of consummation symbolically reflects this blood bond in marriage, uniting two lives into one. During biblical times, people viewed the bride's blood from her first intercourse as a sign of her virginity and the consummation of the marriage covenant. This practice is reflected in Deuteronomy 22:13-17:

> *"If any man takes a wife, and goes in to her, and detests her, and charges her with shameful conduct, and brings a bad name on her, and says, 'I took this woman, and when I came to her I found she was not a virgin,' then the father and mother of the young woman shall take and bring out the evidence of the young woman's virginity to the elders of the city at the gate. And the young woman's father shall say to the elders, 'I gave my daughter to this man as wife, and he detests her. Now he has charged her with shameful conduct, saying, "I found your daughter was not a virgin," and yet these are the evidences of my daughter's virginity.' And they shall spread the cloth before the elders of the city."*

This passage describes a scenario where a husband accuses his new bride of not being a virgin. The bride's family could present the *"evidence of virginity"* (commonly understood as a cloth or sheet stained with blood from the wedding night) to prove her chastity. If the accusation was false, the husband faced punishment; if true, the bride faced severe consequences. This practice shows how culture tied blood to verifying virginity and sealing the marriage covenant in that context. While modern cultures may not emphasize this aspect in the same way, the underlying principle remains: marriage is a covenant that involves a profound, life-altering commitment. The blood bond in marriage, whether symbolic or literal, serves as a reminder that the union is sacred, permanent, and sealed by a commitment that transcends words or legal documents. It is a bond that unites two individuals at the deepest level, reflecting the unity and faithfulness of God's covenants with His people.

MARRIAGE AS AN UNBREAKABLE AGREEMENT

Marriage is intended to be an unbreakable agreement which is central to its identity as a covenant. The Bible is unequivocal in its portrayal of marriage as a lifelong union. In Genesis 2:24 (ESV), we read,

> *"Therefore a man shall leave his father and mother and hold fast to his wife, and they shall become one flesh."*

This *"holding fast"* signifies a permanent bond, one that is not to be broken. Jesus reaffirmed this in Matthew 19:6, stating,

> *"Therefore what God has joined together, let not man separate."*

Here, marriage is not only a human agreement but a divine institution, established and blessed by God Himself. The fact that Jesus warned against breaking the marriage covenant shows that He knows that it can be broken because two imperfect people are committing themselves to each other. The prophet Malachi describes a wife as a, *"companion and wife by covenant,"* (Malachi 2:14)

highlighting the seriousness and permanence of the marital bond. While God ordained marriage, the success of a marriage ultimately depends on the actions and choices of the husband and wife. God's unbreakable role is to provide the foundation, the framework, and the spiritual resources for the covenant to flourish. God's presence as a witness to the marriage covenant elevates it to a sacred status, making it inviolable.

Marriage, as God's sacred design, mirrors the unbreakable nature of His covenants. Just as God did not abandon Israel, despite their idolatry, spouses are called to remain faithful even when the relationship feels strained, seeking reconciliation over dissolution. This is why God hates divorce (Malachi 2:16), it violates the covenant, tearing apart what He has united. Marriage reflects God's faithfulness, calling couples to endure trials and forgive failures, trusting that God, who witnessed their commitment, provides the strength to overcome. In a world where vows are easily discarded, the intent of the marriage covenant to be everlasting stands as a testament to God's enduring design.

MARRIAGE HAS A SACRED OATH

In marriage, the sacred oath is embodied in the wedding vows. These vows are a solemn promise to love, honor, and cherish one another "for better or for worse, in sickness and in health, until death do us part." By speaking these vows before God and witnesses, the couple enters a covenant that is sacred and binding. The significance of the sacred oath in marriage cannot be overstated. It transforms the relationship from a partnership of convenience into a lifelong commitment, rooted in mutual sacrifice and faithfulness. The oath demands that both partners remain true to their promises, even when circumstances become difficult. It serves as a constant reminder that their bond is not contingent on fleeting emotions or personal gain but on a deep, enduring commitment. Life brings challenges, financial strain, illness, conflict, that test a marriage. The covenant's sacred oath calls couples to persevere, mirroring God's faithfulness. Consider a couple facing a crisis, such as infidelity or emotional drift. By honoring their vows, seeking counsel, and rebuilding trust, they prove that the sacred oath can guide them through even the darkest times, weaving their love into the tapestry of God's eternal covenant.

MARRIAGE EMBODIES UNENDING LOYALTY AND FAITHFULNESS

Central to the marriage relationship is the concept of unending loyalty and faithfulness. In God's covenants with humanity, His faithfulness is a defining characteristic. Even when His people are unfaithful, God remains steadfast, as seen in Psalm 89:33 (NIV), where God declared,

> *"But I will not take my love from him, nor will I ever betray my faithfulness."*

This divine commitment underscores the unbreakability of God's covenant despite Israel's failures. In marriage, this unending loyalty and faithfulness are essential. Both partners are called to remain loyal to each other, not only in their actions but also in their hearts and minds. This means honoring the exclusivity of the marriage bond, avoiding infidelity, and nurturing the emotional and spiritual connection that sustains the relationship.

Loyalty in marriage goes beyond fidelity; it involves a deep commitment to the well-being of one's spouse. It means standing by each other in times of hardship, supporting each other through life's challenges, and prioritizing the marriage above other relationships or pursuits. Faithfulness, in this context, is not just about avoiding betrayal but about actively cultivating trust, intimacy, and love. In Ephesians 5:25-27 (NIV), Paul compares marriage to Christ's relationship with the Church, stating,

> *"Husbands, love your wives, just as Christ loved the church and gave himself up for her to make her holy, cleansing her by the washing with*

water through the word, and to present her to himself as a radiant church, without stain or wrinkle or any other blemish, but holy and blameless."

This passage highlights the sacrificial love and enduring bond that should define both marriage and Christ's eternal commitment to the Church, urging spouses to mirror this lifelong dedication. In a culture where loyalty is often conditional and faithfulness is undermined by a myriad of temptations, the biblical call to unending loyalty in marriage is both challenging and counter-cultural. Yet, it is precisely this kind of loyalty that reflects God's character and strengthens the marriage covenant. When couples embrace this principle, they create a relationship that is resilient, trustworthy, and deeply fulfilling, a living testament to the faithfulness of God.

MARRIAGE UNITES A MAN AND A WOMAN

The final characteristic of a covenant is that it unites two parties into a single entity. In biblical covenants, this unity is often symbolized through shared meals, exchanges of names, or other rituals that signify the merging of identities. In the covenant between God and Israel, the people are called to be His,

"treasured possession," (Exodus 19:5, NIV)

set apart and united with Him in a unique relationship. In marriage, this unity is described as two becoming one flesh (Genesis 2:24). This profound statement speaks to the physical, emotional, and spiritual union that marriage creates.

When a man and a woman enter the marriage covenant, they are no longer two separate individuals but a single unit, bound together in a way that is meant to be inseparable. Jesus reinforces this idea in Mark 10:7-9, saying,

"'A man shall leave his father and mother and be joined to his wife, and the two shall become one flesh'; so then they are no longer two, but one flesh.' Therefore what God has joined together, let not man separate."

Here, the unity of marriage is not just a human construct but a divine act, orchestrated by God Himself. This unity has practical implications for how couples live their lives. It means that decisions are made together, all assets are held mutual, and liabilities and responsibilities are shared within the marriage covenant. It also means that the success or failure of one partner affects the other, as they are now intertwined in every aspect of life. This level of unity requires selflessness, compromise, and a willingness to prioritize the needs of the marriage over individual desires. Marriage involves a male and a female, the two becoming one, as God designed from the beginning. In today's individualistic culture, where personal autonomy is often prized above all else, the biblical concept of unity in marriage can be difficult to embrace. Yet, it is this very unity that makes marriage such a powerful reflection of God's covenant with His people, a bond that is meant to endure until death.

Despite the clear biblical teaching on marriage as a covenant, modern culture has increasingly distorted and undermined this sacred institution. We really don't have anything else in our culture to connect with these definitions of an unbreakable agreement, upholding an oath, loyalty, faithfulness, and two becoming one like we'll witness in biblical accounts throughout this book. Perhaps the closest parallel we find is in the obligation of repaying a loan, where the commitment to fulfill a financial contract is often treated as more inviolable than the marriage covenant itself. Unfortunately, marriage has been under assault for so long that we don't even understand this concept in marriage anymore.

One of the most visible signs of this assault is the rising divorce rate. In many societies, divorce has become both acceptable and expected, with couples entering marriage with the mindset that if it doesn't work out, they can simply part ways. This attitude stands in stark contrast to the biblical view of marriage that is intended to be an unbreakable covenant and to last a lifetime. Not only is the divorce rate still on the rise, but our culture has strayed so far that we're okay with things like same-sex marriage. From a biblical perspective, this is a contradiction of terms, it cancels itself out. Marriage, as God designed it, involves a male and a female, the two becoming one, reflecting the complementary nature of His creation.

Satan has skillfully blitzed and blighted the concept of marriage in our culture. It's demonic, an agenda to destroy the home, destroy the concept of marriage, and destroy God's divine design. It's an attempt to destroy covenant itself. Beyond these issues, the broader cultural emphasis on individualism, instant gratification, and personal happiness often clashes with the self-sacrificial nature of covenantal love. In a world where relationships are often viewed through the lens of personal fulfillment, the idea of committing to another person "for better or for worse" can seem outdated or even oppressive. Marriage is supposed to be until death, this concept is lost in our culture, but it's not lost in the Bible or in the heart and mind of God. Yet, it is precisely in this cultural context that the biblical vision of marriage as a covenant shines brightest. By embracing the principles of blood bond, unbreakable agreement, sacred oath, unending loyalty, and unity, couples can create marriages that not only endure but thrive. These marriages serve as a testament to God's faithfulness and a countercultural witness to the power of covenantal love.

COVENANT IN A COVENANT-BREAKING CULTURE

Understanding covenant requires us to confront its stark contrast with today's world. We live in an age where promises are fragile, where loyalty bends under self-interest, and where trust erodes amidst deception. The Bible foresaw this decline. In 2 Timothy 3:1-3 (KJV), Paul warned of the last days:

"Men shall be lovers of their own selves, covetous, boasters, proud, blasphemers, disobedient to parents, unthankful, unholy, without natural affection, trucebreakers."

Romans 1:31 (KJV) reiterates this list and adds,

"covenant breakers,"

to it, painting a picture of a society unmoored from fidelity. Broken marriages, reneged contracts, and discarded commitments litter our cultural landscape, making the steadfastness of God's covenant feel alien.

This backdrop breeds suspicion, even among Christians. All around us people are lying and being deceitful, so we aren't used to the concept of what God can provide us. We have been conditioned to doubt since childhood—parents, teachers, and friends make promises they don't keep, embedding suspicion deep within us. When God speaks, we hesitate, expecting the same disappointment. This is why we struggle so much today to even believe in God's word.

How often do we hear, "Can I really trust God?" or "Why would God do that for me?" Such sentiments betray a heart conditioned by human unfaithfulness, projecting our failings onto God. Yet Scripture counters this doubt emphatically. Even though our world profanes the sacred and dilutes concepts like marriage through cultural assaults, God's covenant remains an unshaken rock. This cultural disconnect challenges us to reframe our understanding. We live in a world of truth breaking, but God wants us to know that he can always be counted on. He is not like us.

A COVENANT AS SURE AS CREATION

To understand the unshakable nature of God's promises, we need to look no further than the rhythm of creation itself, a rhythm He established and upholds as a testament to His faithfulness. The Bible reveals that God ties the certainty of

His promises to the very order of the universe. This is a truth that offers us hope, assurance, and a foundation for faith rooted in His unchanging nature.

In Genesis 1:14-16, God spoke the universe into existence:

"Then God said, 'Let there be lights in the firmament of the heavens to divide the day from the night; and let them be for signs and seasons, and for days and years; and let them be for lights in the firmament of the heavens to give light on the earth'; and it was so. Then God made two great lights: the greater light to rule the day, and the lesser light to rule the night. He made the stars also."

With these words, He flung the stars and galaxies into being and set the sun to rule by day and the moon by night. The sun rises, painting the sky with light, then sets, ushering in darkness. The moon ascends, casting its gentle glow, then fades as the sun returns. This cycle—day in, day out—has rolled on without interruption since the dawn of time. He bound Himself to this rhythm. No force—be it a nuclear bomb, human ingenuity, or demonic power—can disrupt it. God proves His faithfulness in covenant as seen in Jeremiah 33:20-21:

"Thus says the Lord: 'If you can break My covenant with the day and My covenant with the night, so that there will not be day and night in their season, then My covenant may also be broken with David My servant, so that he shall not have a son to reign on his throne.'"

This is a bold divine challenge. God is saying, "If you can break My covenant with day and night, then maybe you can break My promises to you." But you can't. The sun will rise tomorrow morning, the moon will shine tonight, God's word will stand firm, and His promises are unshakable. He has bound Himself to His word with a fidelity that neither will end nor can falter.

This promise to David, a son to reign on his throne forever, finds its perfect fulfillment in Jesus Christ, who now rules from heaven. Like the sun's steady climb each morning, which whispers of tomorrow's certainty, God's covenant stands as a testament to His unwavering faithfulness. That faithfulness stretches beyond David to Abraham and, through Jesus, reaches us today, linking us to an eternal promise that endures as surely as the dawn.

LIVING IN COVENANT CONFIDENCE

Scripture reveals that there are things God *cannot* do, not due to weakness, but because of His perfect nature. Titus 1:2 declares,

> *"In hope of eternal life which God, who cannot lie, promised before time began."*

God *cannot* lie. This isn't a choice; it's an impossibility rooted in His essence. If He spoke a falsehood, it would become truth by the power of His word, such is His holiness.

But lying isn't the only thing beyond Him. God cannot sin, He doesn't even know the impulse to sin, for He is utterly holy. He cannot change, as Hebrews 13:8 affirms:

> *"Jesus Christ is the same yesterday, today, and forever."*

These "limitations" are not flaws; they are the bedrock of His reliability. Most crucially, God cannot break His word. Psalm 119:89 reinforces this:

> *"Forever, O Lord, Your word is settled in heaven."*

When God makes a promise, He binds Himself to it with His unchanging character.

Unlike us, who falter despite good intentions, God's word is unbreakable. In these last days, where trucebreakers and covenant breakers abound, God's covenant remains our lifeline. It's not just about witnessing His acts—like the Israelites who saw miracles yet missed His heart (Psalm 103:7)—but knowing His ways, His unchanging faithfulness. This knowledge dispels suspicion, replacing it with trust. Knowing that we can trust in God and believe this fully in our hearts will further unwrap the secret of the Lord in our lives. As the sun rises each morning, we're reminded: God keeps His word. As the moon glows each night, we're assured: His covenant endures.

TEN RITUALS OF COVENANT MAKING

The next five chapters will discuss the ten rituals of covenant making. In order to understand the secret of the Lord, we need to understand how covenants are created. Not every ritual is performed in every covenant. However, God has established these as ways to enter into covenant. In your personal Bible study, when you come across these rituals, think covenant and how they apply to the New Covenant God established for believers today.

RITUAL 1 – THE ACT OF CUTTING

RITUAL 2 – PERMANENT SCARRING

RITUAL 3 – CUTTING ANIMALS IN HALF

RITUAL 4 – COVENANT HEADS

RITUAL 5 – THE EXCHANGE OF NAMES

RITUAL 6 – THE EXCHANGE OF BELTS OR GIRDLES

RITUAL 7 – THE EXCHANGE OF GARMENTS

RITUAL 8 – READING THE TERMS

RITUAL 9 – TREES AND STONES AS MEMORIALS

RITUAL 10 – SHARING A MEAL

CHAPTER 4

CUTTING COVENANTS

The scars of Jesus Christ stand as the most profound testament to God's covenant faithfulness in all of Scripture. While no description of Jesus' appearance is provided at the time of His crucifixion, Isaiah 52:14 (NIV) prophesied the harrowing extent of His suffering, declaring,

> *"Just as there were many who were appalled at him—his appearance was so disfigured beyond that of any human being and his form marred beyond human likeness."*

This brutal reality, foretold centuries earlier, reveals that, on the cross, Jesus was marred beyond recognition, His form so distorted that He no longer resembled a human being. This starkly contrasts with the sanitized artistic depictions of the crucifixion common throughout Christian history. No painting or sculpture can truly capture the horror of what Christ endured, yet His scars embody the unbreakable commitment of God's covenant, fulfilled through His sacrificial love.

Yet in His resurrection, God demonstrated His power by healing and glorifying Jesus' broken body. Although God healed His body, scars and holes remained in place as eternal witnesses. The holes in His wrists where nails had pierced, the gash in His side from the Roman spear, and the wounds in His feet were preserved even in His glorified state.

This deliberate preservation of Christ's scars becomes clear in His interaction with Thomas after the resurrection. In John 20:27 when Thomas doubted, Jesus specifically invited him to place his fingers in the holes in His hands and thrust his hand into the wound in His side. These wounds remained as tangible proof of Christ's identity and sacrifice.

This raises an important question: If God chose to heal and glorify Jesus' body, why didn't He heal these specific wounds? Why leave any scars at all on His resurrected Son? The answer reveals a profound truth about God's covenant nature. These scars remain as an eternal reminder of how humanity obtained salvation. They stand as permanent witnesses to the price paid for sin and the depth of God's love for His people. For all eternity, the marks of the covenant will be visible in the glorified body of Christ, testifying to the means by which God redeemed humanity to Himself.

To fully grasp the significance of biblical covenants, one must understand the ancient customs and practices that defined covenant relationships. The phrase "cutting a covenant" may strike us as strange, perhaps even unsettling. In our modern world the idea of shedding blood to seal a deal feels archaic, or tribal in a sense. Yet, in biblical times, it was a sacred act, universally recognized across cultures as the ultimate expression of commitment.

As we learned previously, the Hebrew word for covenant, *berith*, means "to cut till bleeding occurs." This described a physical reality. Blood, as Leviticus 17:11 declares, is life itself, and by spilling it, covenant partners declared, "My life is tied to this promise. I'd rather die than break it." In an era where trust was fragile and betrayal lurked around every corner, cutting a covenant forged a bond that words alone could never secure.

Why would God, the all-powerful Creator, choose such a raw and tangible method to forge a bond with humanity? The answer rests in His heart. Far from a distant sovereign, issuing decrees from on high, God is a relational being who longs for intimacy with us as seen when He walked with Adam in the cool of the garden (Genesis 3:8). Sin shattered that closeness, creating a divide that only blood, the surrender of life, could bridge. Through covenant, God extends a path to restoration, a bridge built on sacrifice, culminating in the cross where Jesus' blood sealed the New Covenant, uniting us to Him in grace for eternity.

This chapter introduces two of ten customs of covenant-making—cutting and scarring—with the remaining eight explored in subsequent chapters. Each custom reveals not only how covenants were formed but why they hold profound significance for both God and humanity. Not every ritual appears in every covenant; rather, these are practices humanity has embraced across time to secure the covenantal promise.

RITUAL 1 – THE ACT OF CUTTING

The first ritual or custom of covenants is the way the cut was done. At the heart of ancient covenant-making lies the act of cutting the body, a ritual where blood is spilled to symbolize the mingling of lives between partners. This practice, foundational across cultures, rested on the belief that blood represents life itself, and by shedding it, those entering a covenant surrendered their very existence to the agreement, forging bonds of loyalty and trust that transcended words. From the sacred rites of the Bible to the diverse customs of ancient civilizations and tribes, the act of cutting took various forms, each a solemn vow etched in flesh, reflecting a universal human need for alliance sealed in lifeblood.

In biblical tradition, covenant-making often involved acts of cutting typically through animal sacrifices (as seen in Genesis 15 where God instructed Abraham to cut animals in half) rather than human blood. Deuteronomy 14:1 states,

> *"You are the children of the Lord your God; you shall not cut your-selves."*

Through this verse, God was prohibiting self-inflicted cuttings tied to pagan mourning or idolatrous rituals, which were common among surrounding nations. These acts were distinct from circumcision, established in Genesis 17 as a sacred sign of God's covenant with Abraham's descendants. Unlike the forbidden cuttings, which were rooted in superstition and false worship, circumcision was a divinely commanded act, marking Israel's identity and obedience with a permanent, physical symbol of their unique bond with God. This act of cutting the foreskin was not about self-harm, but about sealing a spiritual commitment, reflecting the lifeblood of covenant loyalty.

Beyond the biblical world, ancient civilizations and tribes developed their own rituals of cutting and blood-mingling, often involving the direct shedding of human blood to seal covenants. These practices varied widely but shared a common purpose: to create bonds as strong as kinship, where loyalty was cemented in lifeblood.

One widespread method was cutting the palm, where two individuals would slice their hands with a blade and clasp them together, allowing their blood to mingle. This ritual, a precursor to the modern handshake, carried profound significance in ancient times, symbolizing a covenantal promise upheld at great personal cost. The mingling of blood represented a binding commitment, tying the lives of the covenant partners together in a bond of loyalty and trust. Psalm 15:4 celebrates this covenantal integrity, praising the one,

"who swears to his own hurt and does not change."

A carpenter in the early 1900's might pledge to build a barn for five-hundred dollars, and even if costs doubled, he'd complete the work without complaint, his handshake sealed the commitment. In contrast, today's broken agreements often leave projects abandoned and trust fractured, with calls unanswered and questions lingering. Yet the original handshake endures as a quiet echo of a higher standard—a loyalty forged in blood, reflecting an era when people were bound to their word.

Another method, familiar from childhood games, involved cutting or pricking the finger. Two individuals would press their bleeding fingers together, declaring themselves "blood brothers." Though simple, this act carried the full weight of covenant, establishing a bond stronger than natural family ties. In the Middle East, there is a saying, "Blood is thicker than milk," meaning a covenant partner, united by blood, outranks even siblings who shared the same mother's milk. While two brothers might share the same mother's milk creating a natural family bond, a blood covenant creates an even deeper connection. The mingling of blood in covenant establishes a relationship that supersedes natural family ties, creating obligations and loyalties that stand above all other human relationships.

Other examples of blood covenants include the nomadic Scyths of Central Asia in 8th to 4th century BC, as recorded by Herodotus. They wounded themselves with a knife or awl, letting their blood drip into a bowl of wine. Both parties then drank the mixture while invoking their gods, sealing their oath through shared consumption. This ritual, often used for alliances, reflected the Scyths' need for trust in their harsh environment.

In the 9th century, Hungarian tribes engaged in blood oaths. The seven tribal leaders cut their arms and let their blood mix in a chalice, becoming blood brothers. This ritual was considered the first unwritten constitution of the Hungarian nation, aimed at uniting the tribes before their migration into the Carpathian basin. It underscores the importance of blood as a unifying force in tribal politics.

Various African tribes, particularly in east-central Africa, like those in Rwanda, practiced blood pacts. These pacts involved parties shedding blood into a container, which might be drunk or used to sign a document. This practice reflected the cultural importance of blood as a symbol of life and commitment, making it suitable for serious agreements.

In the Philippines, the Visayan people and other tribes practiced "sandugo" or blood compact, a ritual documented during Spanish colonization. This involved cutting hands and pouring blood into a cup of wine, which was then drunk by both parties. A famous instance was the 1565 pact between Miguel López de Legazpi and Datu Sikatuna of Bohol, symbolizing peace and friendship. This practice was used to seal treaties and friendships, highlighting its diplomatic role.

These rituals reveal a shared understanding: blood was the ultimate currency of trust, transforming promises into sacred obligations. The serious nature of these bonds explains why their violation often led to severe consequences—wars erupted, and conflicts persisted for generations over broken covenants. Modern society struggles to grasp this depth, but in ancient times, a covenant was a lifeline. The diversity of methods—from communal drinking in Scythian and Philippine rituals to the chalice-mixing of Hungarian tribes—reflects cultural and environmental influences, yet the core symbolism of life and commitment remained constant. When God enters covenant with us, blood remains central. From the animal sacrifices of Genesis to the cross of Calvary, it's the life given up that binds us to Him, a reminder that covenant isn't a light commitment but a bond unto death.

RITUAL 2 – PERMANENT SCARRING

Once the cut was made, the covenant ritual advanced with a vital step: they ensured the wound left a lasting scar. This act deliberately crafted a permanent mark, a visible testament to the covenant that endured as a constant reminder for both the partners and their communities.

There are several instances where permanent marks are used to remember God's covenant. In Genesis 17:11-14, God commands Abraham to circumcise himself and all males in his household as a sign of the covenant. This act leaves a permanent scar on the body, symbolizing a lifelong commitment to God. In John 20:27, after His resurrection, Christ shows His disciples the scars from His crucifixion, saying to Thomas,

> *"Put your finger here, and see my hands; and put out your hand, and place it in my side. Do not disbelieve, but believe."*

These eternal scars are a testament to the new covenant sealed by His blood, serving as a permanent reminder.

Beyond the biblical narrative, ancient civilizations across the globe employed scarification to create lasting reminders of commitments, alliances, and identity, often enhancing the process with ashes or similar materials. The purpose of creating a lasting scar went beyond a ceremonial ritual. When tribal chiefs entered covenant with one another, the permanent mark served as a visible testimony to their own people of their sacred obligations. As they walked among their respective tribes, the scar reminded both them and their people of the binding agreement between the two communities. This visible mark declared that the chief had pledged his life and the lives of his people to maintain faithfulness to the covenant relationship.

These permanent marks of covenant demonstrate an important biblical principle: God considers covenant relationships worthy of lasting remembrance. Just as tribal chiefs bore scars that testified to their covenant obligations, Christ's scars eternally testify to His covenant faithfulness toward His people. For countless generations to come, these marks will stand as reminders of how salvation was purchased through the shedding of blood and the establishment of an everlasting covenant.

The practice of creating permanent covenant scars reflected the understanding that these agreements were meant to last beyond the immediate moment of their making. They were intended to bind not only the current generation but future generations as well. The visible scar served as a constant reminder that breaking the covenant would mean death, as the participants had pledged their very lives in the making of the agreement.

These ancient covenant practices of cutting and scarring illuminate the significance of Christ's crucifixion. When Jesus was marred beyond recognition on the cross, His body bore the cuts and scars of the ultimate covenant sacrifice. Though God raised Him with a glorified body, He chose to preserve the holes and scars in Jesus' hands, feet, and side. Every cross we see, every communion cup we lift, calls us back to that moment when love was carved into His hands, feet, and side. These eternal marks serve as a testament to the new covenant established through His blood and act as a reminder to all Christians of the new covenant.

CHAPTER 5

CUTTING ANIMALS IN HALF

RITUAL 3 – CUTTING ANIMALS IN HALF

In the Bible, the practice of cutting animals in half during covenant making was a solemn and symbolic ritual. Cutting animals in half was a common way to formalize agreements. The divided animals made the covenant tangible and vivid, leaving a lasting impression on those who participated. The shedding of blood also played a crucial role as blood represents life. By spilling the animals' blood, the participants underscored that the covenant was a matter of utmost seriousness—a bond sealed with life itself. This made the agreement sacred and binding, often under the watchful eyes of divine witnesses.

The primary reason for cutting animals in half was to symbolize the gravity of the covenant and the consequences of breaking it. By arranging the animal halves and walking (or having a divine symbol pass) between them, the parties were making a self-maledictory oath. This meant they were saying, "May this happen to me if I break this covenant." In other words, "May I be torn apart like these animals if I fail to keep my promise." The ritual invoked a curse upon the covenant breaker, tying the agreement to a life-and-death commitment. While we may view the ritual as harsh, it was a powerful and meaningful act in its time, conveying the weight of the promises made.

We will cover two stories of cutting animals in half from the Bible. In Genesis 15, the ritual takes on a profound theological meaning. Notably, Abram does not walk between the pieces, only God does, symbolized by the smoking oven and burning torch. This signifies that God is binding Himself to the covenant unilaterally and demonstrates God's unwavering faithfulness and commitment to His people, emphasizing that the covenant's success depends entirely on His reliability, not human effort.

By contrast, human failure to uphold covenants is highlighted elsewhere. In Jeremiah 34:18-20, the people of Judah cut a calf in half and walked between its parts to vow the release of their Hebrew slaves. When they later break this promise by re-enslaving them, God warns that they will face the fate they invoked: being torn apart like the calf. This shows the ritual's dual purpose, both as a pledge of loyalty and a warning of consequences.

The ritual also carries deeper significance in biblical theology. The cutting of animals in half foreshadows the ultimate covenant established through Jesus Christ. Just as the animals were divided to seal earlier covenants, Jesus' body was broken and His blood shed on the cross to establish the New Covenant as Hebrews 9:22 (ESV) states,

"Without the shedding of blood, there is no forgiveness of sins."

His sacrifice fulfills the pattern of blood sealing a covenant, offering eternal reconciliation between God and humanity.

GENESIS 15: GOD'S COVENANT WITH ABRAM

In Genesis 15, the chapter opens with God's promise to Abram:

"Do not be afraid, Abram. I am your shield, your exceedingly great reward." (v.1)

Abram, childless and aging, responds with a question born of both faith and longing:

> *"Lord God, what will You give me, seeing I go childless, and the heir of my house is Eliezer of Damascus?"* (v.2)

God reassures him, promising a son from his own body and descendants as numerous as the stars (vv.4-5). Yet Abram presses further:

> *"Lord God, how shall I know that I will inherit it?"* (v.8)

Abram is not doubting God's word so much as seeking confirmation, a tangible sign that this vast promise, of a son and a land, will come to pass. God's response is striking. He instructs Abram,

> *"Bring Me a three-year-old heifer, a three-year-old female goat, a three-year-old ram, a turtledove, and a young pigeon."* (v.9)

Without further direction, Abram acts instinctively:

> *"Then he brought all these to Him and cut them in two, down the middle, and placed each piece opposite the other; but he did not cut the birds in two."* (v.10)

As the sun sets, a deep sleep falls upon Abram, and in a vision,

> *"a smoking oven, and a burning torch that passed between those pieces."* (v.17)

In that moment, God seals the covenant, promising the land to Abram's seed and foretelling their sojourn in Egypt (vv.13-16, 18-21).

These animals all serve a different purpose. In biblical sacrifices, the heifer holds significant symbolic weight, primarily associated with purification and cleansing from sin. The heifer's role is most vividly seen in Numbers 19 where the issue of ritual impurity is addressed for Israelites participating in Tabernacle worship and communal activities. The primary concern in Numbers 19 is impurity resulting from contact with a human corpse, considered one of the most severe forms of defilement in ancient Israelite law. Such impurity could arise from touching a dead body, being in a tent where someone died, or even handling bones or graves (Numbers 19:11-16). This impurity lasted seven days and required a specific purification process to restore the individual to a state of ritual purity, allowing them to rejoin the community and approach God's presence without defiling the sanctuary. In the case of Abram, the heifer symbolically cleanses him before being in God's presence.

The female goat is a key sacrificial animal in the Bible, predominantly linked to sin atonement, particularly in the Day of Atonement (Yom Kippur) ritual. Leviticus 16 outlines the Day of Atonement, a pivotal annual ritual in ancient Israel designed to atone for the sins of the entire community, including the priests, the people, and the sanctuary itself. Central to this ritual are two goats, one of which is a female goat used as a sin offering for the people, and the other, known as the "scapegoat," which symbolically carries the sins of Israel into the wilderness. The female goat's blood cleanses Abram of any sins before the covenant ritual.

The ram holds profound significance in biblical sacrifices, embodying substitution and complete dedication to God, making it a vital symbol in covenant and worship. This meaning deepens later in Abraham's life in Genesis 22, where God tests his loyalty by commanding the sacrifice of his son Isaac, the long-awaited heir promised in Genesis 15. Abraham's willingness to offer Isaac demonstrates his fear of the Lord and total devotion, but God intervenes, providing a ram caught in a thicket to sacrifice in Isaac's place. This act of substitution prefigures God's redemptive provision, culminating in Christ's sacrifice. In Genesis 15:9, the ram's role in the covenant ritual mirrors this theme of substitution. God intends to establish a covenant with Abram, yet substitutes him in the ritual, passing alone as a smoking oven (God the Father) and a burning torch (God the Son) through the divided animals in Genesis 15:17. The ram, cut in half to form the blood-soaked path, underscores the covenant's gravity and God's unilateral commitment, foreshadowing the ultimate substitutionary atonement through Christ.

Alongside the heifer, female goat, and ram, God instructs Abram to include a turtle dove and a young pigeon in the covenant ritual of Genesis 15:9. Unlike the larger animals, which are cut in half to underscore the covenant's grave commitment, the birds remain undivided, symbolizing wholeness and unity. This suggests that God's promise encompasses all of Abram's descendants, with no part excluded. Their presence complements the larger animals, creating a comprehensive offering that blends material blessings (represented by the heifer, female goat, and ram) with spiritual dimensions (embodied by the birds), reflecting the covenant's promise of both land and lineage. By leaving the birds whole, they likely signify life, preservation, and the enduring nature of God's pledge, contrasting with the divided animals' emphasis on sacrifice and cost. Thus, the turtle dove and young pigeon highlight the covenant's life-giving and sustaining essence, affirming God's commitment to fulfill His promise through Abram's descendants.

The ritual of cutting animals in half to forge a covenant reveals the profound faithfulness of God, starkly contrasted with human frailty. The lifeless animal halves, arranged to form a blood-soaked path, served as a vivid reminder that breaking the covenant would bring a fate as certain as the animals' death, a curse of destruction upon the covenant breaker. This grim symbolism underscores why God put Abram to sleep, rendering him a passive observer as divine symbols, a smoking oven and burning torch, passed through the pieces alone. Abram awakens to join this covenant by faith, not by participating in the ritual, highlighting that its fulfillment depends solely on God's promise.

Without understanding the language of covenant, this scene might perplex us. Yet, through the lens of covenant, it becomes a portrait of God's unyielding faithfulness, a promise so secure that He stakes His own existence on it. This divine reliability stands in sharp contrast to human fallibility, where man can falter in keeping their covenant commitments as seen in Jeremiah 34.

JEREMIAH 34: ZEDEKIAH WARNED BY GOD

Jeremiah 34 occurs in the shadow of impending doom. King Zedekiah was the last monarch of Judah, which was comprised of the tribes of Judah and Benjamin, along with a portion of the tribe of Levi and remnants of other tribes who may have fled to Judah after Assyrian conquest of the northern Kingdom of Israel. He was appointed by the Babylonians and ruled a fractured kingdom plagued by idolatry, injustice, and foreign domination. The prophet Jeremiah, imprisoned for his unflinching warnings, receives a word from God condemning Zedekiah's fate (vv.1-7) before shifting to a covenantal scandal involving slavery (vv.8-22).

At the heart of Jeremiah 34 is the enslavement of fellow Hebrews by the people of Judah themselves, a violation of God's covenantal law established in the Torah. According to Deuteronomy 15:12-15 and Exodus 21:2-6, if a Hebrew (an Israelite) sold himself into servitude due to poverty or debt, he was to serve for no more than six years before being released with provisions, as a reminder of Israel's own liberation from Egyptian bondage. This law was rooted in God's lovingkindness, ensuring that His people treated one another with mercy and justice, reflecting the covenantal bond they shared as kin under Yahweh.

However, in Judah, the elite—princes, priests, officials, and wealthy landowners—had flagrantly ignored this command. They perpetuated indefinite slavery among their own brethren, exploiting fellow Israelites for economic gain in a war-torn economy. These "slaves" were not foreigners but Hebrew men and women from the tribes of Judah and Benjamin, bound by blood and covenant to the same God. King Zedekiah, along with the leaders and people, convened in

Jerusalem to address this longstanding sin, proclaiming a covenant to free every Hebrew slave.

They solemnized this vow in the temple, cutting a calf in half and walking between its severed parts—a ritual invoking a self-curse: "May we be torn apart like this animal if we break our word" (echoing Genesis 15). This was a public declaration with participants ranging from royalty, priests, officials, and commoners witnessed by God and the community, binding all levels of Judah's society to the same fate. Unlike Genesis 15, where God alone bore the covenant's weight, here the people of Judah took responsibility, invoking both the promise and the peril upon themselves.

Initially, they complied and freed the slaves. This liberation was a radical restoration of justice, carrying deep legal and spiritual significance, aimed at aligning Judah with God's will and securing His protection. It also bolstered national unity against the Babylonians by freeing able-bodied men to fight. Yet, when the siege lifted briefly, complacency set in. The same leaders and people,

> *"changed their minds and made the male and female slaves return, whom they had set free, and brought them into subjection as male and female slaves."* (v.11)

They re-enslaved those they had freed, desecrating the ritual's sanctity and betraying both their kin and their God. The reasons for this reversal are complex: economic pressures in a war-ravaged land may have driven them to reclaim their labor force, the temporary relief from danger might have bred complacency, or their initial repentance may have been insincere, a calculated act lacking true conviction. Whatever the cause, their actions turned a sacred pledge into a hollow gesture, and the blood that had united them now stood as a witness against them.

Their betrayal desecrated the covenant, profaning God's name (v.16) and mocking the liberty He had granted Israel at the Exodus. God's response, delivered through Jeremiah, was swift and resolute. He reminded them of the ritual they had enacted and the law they had sworn to uphold. By breaking the covenant, they had triggered its inherent curse:

> *"I will make them like the calf which they cut in two and passed between its parts."* (v.18, ESV)

Their fate would mirror the animal's—torn apart, their bodies left unburied as prey for birds and beasts and delivered into the hands of the Babylonians.

This "tearing apart" was prophesied in earlier chapters of Jeremiah where Judah's unfaithfulness invites Babylonian swords and the scavenging of beasts. In Jeremiah 19:7 (NIV), God declares,

> *"In this place I will ruin the plans of Judah and Jerusalem; I will make them fall by the sword before their enemies...and I will give their carcasses as food for the birds and the wild animals."*

Similar echoes appear in Jeremiah 15:3 (NIV),

> *"I will send four kinds of destroyers against them...the sword to kill and the dogs to drag away and the birds and the wild animals to devour and destroy."*

Also Jeremiah 7:33 (NIV),

> *"Then the carcasses of this people will become food for the birds and the wild animals."*

These prophecies painted a consistent picture of Judah's fragmentation—torn by invasion, exile, and nature's predators—as fulfillment of covenant curses. This judgment was a direct reflection of the ritual's symbolism, a fulfillment of the self-imposed curse they had invoked.

As prophecy came to fruition, the consequences were devastating. In 586 BC, Jerusalem fell to Nebuchadnezzar's forces. Its walls were breached, its temple razed, and its people exiled. Zedekiah, who had walked between the calf's halves, was captured, forced to witness his sons' execution, blinded, and led in chains to Babylon. The broken covenant had unleashed a torrent of destruction, confirming the grim prophecy embedded in the ritual.

The events of Jeremiah 34 carry enduring lessons. They highlight the gravity of biblical covenants where violation invites severe repercussions. The ritual's blood and division also foreshadow the ultimate covenant in Christ's sacrifice, where His blood establishes an unbreakable bond between God and humanity (Hebrews 9:15). Unlike Judah's failure, Jesus' faithfulness ensures eternal redemption, transforming the old covenants' curse into the new covenant's grace.

OTHER HISTORICAL ACCOUNTS

Historical accounts suggests that the practice of cutting animals in half for covenant making was not unique to the Bible but was a widespread custom in the ancient Near East, spanning regions like Mesopotamia, Syria, Turkey, and Assyria. This is evidenced by archaeological discoveries and ancient texts uncovered over the last century, which provide insight into the historical and cultural contexts of these rituals. The evidence leans toward this being a common practice among different societies, speaking various languages, and lasting for hundreds of years. It seems likely that this ritual was part of a broader cultural tradition where covenants were sealed with solemn, tangible acts to ensure binding agreements, often invoking divine witnesses to enforce terms.

The practice is particularly documented in the second and first millennia BC, periods roughly equivalent to the time from Abraham to King David and from King David to Christ, respectively. These timeframes align with significant biblical events, suggesting a shared cultural milieu where such rituals were understood and practiced. The cultural prevalence is supported by findings from sites like Mari (modern Syria), Alalakh (modern Turkey), and Hittite territories, indicating that the ritual was not isolated to Israel but was a regional norm.

THE ROLE OF BLOOD

At the heart of cutting animals in half lies blood, the life force that seals the covenant. Leviticus 17:11 ties blood to life explicitly, stating,

> *"For the life of the flesh is in the blood, and I have given it to you upon the altar to make atonement for your souls; for it is the blood that makes atonement for the soul."*

In ancient covenant-making, shedding blood was essential. Whether through the sacrifice of animals or in the cutting of participants' own flesh, blood symbolized the total surrender of life to the agreement. This is why the Hebrew word *berith* is linked to cutting until blood flows, the covenant demanded life itself. The act of dividing animals, their blood pooling between the halves, was a visceral testament to the gravity of the commitment, a promise written in the currency of life.

This role of blood reverberates through Scripture, finding its fullest expression in the New Covenant. At the Last Supper, Jesus lifts the cup and declares,

> *"This cup is the new covenant in My blood, which is shed for you."*
> (Luke 22:20)

His crucifixion, where His blood pours out upon the cross, mirrors the ancient ritual but surpasses it infinitely. The animals in Genesis pointed to a greater sacrifice, one where God Himself, in the person of Christ, becomes the offering. Hebrews 9:22 states unequivocally,

"Without shedding of blood there is no remission."

This verse links blood inextricably to atonement. Christ's death doesn't just seal the covenant; it redeems us, binding us to God with a life poured out not by us, but for us. The Roman spear piercing His side, releasing blood and water (John 19:34), echoes the split carcasses of Genesis, but now the blood is divine, the life eternal.

The covenant with Abram in Genesis 15 is a thread woven into God's redemptive tapestry. The promise of a son leads to Isaac, the land to Canaan, and the descendants to Israel—and ultimately to Jesus, the seed through whom,

"all the families of the earth shall be blessed." (Genesis 12:3)

The ritual of cutting animals prefigures the cross, where Christ's body is broken and His blood shed to establish the New Covenant. Hebrews 10:10 proclaims,

"We have been sanctified through the offering of the body of Jesus Christ once for all."

The animal halves in Genesis are a type and a shadow of Calvary. Yet, the parallels deepen: just as the vultures descended on the carcasses and Abram drove them away (Genesis 15:11), so too did darkness and death encroach at the cross, only to be overcome by Christ's triumph. The ancient ritual, with its blood and division, whispers of a sacrifice that would one day silence the curse of sin.

This connection transforms how we see Genesis 15. God's solitary walk between the pieces foreshadows His solitary work on the cross. Just as Abram entered the covenant by faith, trusting God's promise despite his own inability, we enter the New Covenant through faith in Christ's finished work. The path between the animal halves traced a figure-eight, an infinity symbol, representing the eternal nature of the bond. That eternity finds its fulfillment in the everlasting life secured not by our strength but by His sacrifice. When Jesus cries,

"It is finished" (John 19:30),

He completes the covenant God swore by Himself, ensuring that nothing, not sin or death, can break it. The blood of animals could only point forward; the blood of Christ accomplishes what they could not, reconciling humanity to God in an unbreakable union.

Consider the profound mystery embedded in these acts of blood and covenant when unraveling the secret of the Lord. The ritual of cutting animals, with its flowing blood and solemn vows, peels back the veil on God's unwavering faithfulness and the staggering cost of redemption. It reveals that covenant is not a casual pact but a life-bound promise, secured by the very life of God Himself. While humanity's covenants falter, as seen in Israel's failures in Jeremiah 34, God's stands unyielding, sealed in the blood of animals in Genesis and fulfilled in the blood of Christ on the cross. To grasp this is to glimpse the secret of the Lord: a love so fierce it bleeds, a commitment so steadfast it dies, and a promise so eternal it rises again. Through the lens of split carcasses and a crucified Savior, we see not just an ancient practice, but the pulsing, bleeding heart of God, a heart that pours out life to claim us as His own, forever.

CHAPTER 6

COVENANT HEADS

RITUAL 4 – COVENANT HEADS

In the pages of Scripture, a remarkable pattern emerges: the actions of a single individual often carry weight far beyond their own life, shaping the destiny of families, nations, or even all humanity. These individuals, known as "covenant heads," step into sacred agreements with God, acting as representatives whose decisions, whether faithful or rebellious, bind those they stand for. Rooted in ancient covenant-making customs, where blood and oaths forged bonds, this divine design reveals a communal reality. Yet, it is through this lens that God chooses to relate to us, unfolding His redemptive story across generations.

At its core, a covenant head is more than a leader or a hero; they are a conduit of God's will, their choices rippling outward to bring blessing or curse. This chapter invites you into this profound concept, tracing its thread through the biblical narrative. We begin with Adam, whose disobedience in Eden plunged humanity into sin, and journey through pivotal figures like Noah, whose ark preserved life. We will look at Phinehas, whose zeal secured a priesthood, Abraham, whose faith birthed a nation, David, whose victories liberated Israel, and Jonathan, whose covenant love extended grace to the broken. Each story builds toward the ultimate covenant head, Jesus Christ, whose perfect obedience restores what was lost and invites us into an eternal promise.

You might wonder: why does God allow one person's actions to affect so many? This question strikes at the heart of *federal headship*—a principle where humanity is interconnected, not isolated. It may seem unfair that Adam's fall stains us all or that David's triumph frees a nation. Yet, as we'll see, this is the framework through which God coordinates His plan of redemption, culminating in Jesus, who stands as our flawless representative. Through Him, the consequences of human failure are overturned, and we are drawn into a relationship secured not by our own merits, but by His unwavering faithfulness.

As we explore these covenant heads, we'll wrestle with their implications—questions of responsibility, representation, and grace—and uncover how their roles illuminate our own place in God's family. From the garden to the cross, this chapter reveals a narrative of interconnected destinies, where the faithfulness of a few reshapes the future of many. Most importantly, it points us to Christ, the head who binds us to God's eternal covenant, offering a seat at His table that we could never earn.

ADAM: THE FIRST COVENANT HEAD

In the verdant paradise of Eden, God placed Adam, the first man, as a covenant head, a representative whose choices would shape the destiny of all who followed. As detailed in Genesis 2:15-17, God entrusted Adam with the care of the garden and issued a clear command:

> *"Of every tree of the garden you may freely eat; but of the tree of the knowledge of good and evil you shall not eat, for in the day that you eat of it you shall surely die."*

This wasn't a private directive for Adam alone; it established a covenantal relationship where he stood as the head of all humanity. Every person who would ever live had, in a spiritual sense ("in Adam"), their fate tied to his obedience or rebellion.

When temptation slithered into Eden through the serpent's cunning words,

> *"Did God really say 'You shall not eat of any tree in the garden?'"*
> (Genesis 3:1, NIV),

Eve faced a pivotal moment. Deceived by the serpent's crafty questioning, she ate of the forbidden fruit, and Adam, though not deceived, chose to follow, eating as well (Genesis 3:6 and 1 Timothy 2:14). As the covenant head, Adam's deliberate disobedience bore universal consequences, fracturing the harmony of creation. The Apostle Paul captures this stark reality in Romans 5:12:

> *"Therefore, just as through one man sin entered the world, and death through sin, and thus death spread to all men, because all sinned."*

Through Adam's choice, sin and death surged into existence, staining every human heart and severing our direct communion with God. It's as if we were all present in that garden, bound by Adam's decision, inheriting a legacy of brokenness we didn't choose.

This raises a troubling question: Why are we held accountable for Adam's sin? It feels profoundly unfair, why should we suffer for a choice made thousands of years ago by someone else? The answer lies in the nature of covenantal representation. A covenant head acts on behalf of those they represent, their actions rippling outward to affect the entire group. Think of a king declaring war: his decision thrusts his people into conflict, whether they wield a sword or not. Similarly, Adam's rebellion plunged humanity into spiritual ruin, leaving us spiritually crippled, our "legs" broken, unable to walk into God's presence unaided. This doctrine, often called original sin, explains why rebellion feels innate, why we stray even before we consciously choose to. We didn't eat the fruit, but as part of Adam's posterity, we bear its bitter consequences.

Yet, amid this tragedy, a thread of hope emerges. Adam's failure isn't the final chapter; it's the prelude to redemption. Even as the curse fell in Eden, God whispered a promise in Genesis 3:15: a descendant would one day crush the serpent's head, hinting at a savior who would reverse the damage. This points to Jesus, the ultimate covenant head, who succeeded where Adam faltered. Adam's disobedience forfeited a perfect life, but Jesus restores it. Paul reinforces this in 1 Corinthians 15:22:

"For as in Adam all die, so in Christ all shall be made alive."

Through Jesus' perfect obedience, the fracture Adam caused begins to heal.

Adam's role as the first covenant head sets the stage for the Bible's unfolding narrative. Scripture reveals other covenant heads—Noah, whose obedience preserved humanity through the flood, Abraham, whose faith birthed a nation of blessing, Moses, who delivered Israel from bondage, and David, whose throne foreshadowed the Messiah. Each represents their people, their actions shaping destinies. But all these figures point to Jesus, the flawless covenant head. Where Adam brought death, Jesus brings life; where Adam disobeyed, Jesus fulfilled every command. Adam's story, then, is our story, it explains our brokenness and our need for redemption. His fall underscores the devastating power of a covenant head's failure, yet it also unveils God's relentless grace, culminating in Christ, who invites us back to the table we lost in Eden, not by our merit, but by His unwavering faithfulness.

NOAH: A COVENANT HEAD FOR ALL CREATION

Long before the rise of Israel's patriarchs or kings, Noah emerged as a pivotal figure in God's redemptive plan, a covenant head whose obedience preserved life amidst a world consumed by corruption. In the antediluvian era, humanity had spiraled into moral decay, their hearts steeped in violence and sin. Yet, amid this darkness, Noah stood apart, described as, *"a just man, perfect in his generations"* (Genesis 6:9).

God chose Noah and gave him an extraordinary task: building an ark to be a vessel of salvation. Through this act of faith, Noah became the representative not only of his family but of all creation, securing their survival through the cataclysmic flood that would soon engulf the earth. When the waters receded and the ark rested on Mount Ararat, God established a covenant with Noah, a sacred promise that extended far beyond one man to encompass all living things and future generations.

The covenant God made with Noah after the flood is remarkable for its breadth. God declared,

> *"I establish My covenant with you: Never again shall all flesh be cut off by the waters of the flood; never again shall there be a flood to destroy the earth."* (Genesis 9:11)

This promise was not limited to Noah and his immediate family; it included,

> *"every living creature of all flesh,"* (Genesis 9:15)

from the birds of the air to the beasts of the field. As a sign of this covenant, God set the rainbow in the sky, a symbol of His mercy and faithfulness, ensuring that the earth would never again face such total destruction. Noah's role as covenant head thus positioned him as the linchpin through whom God reaffirmed His commitment to sustain creation, offering a new beginning after the judgment.

Noah's role extended beyond the ark's construction and the flood's aftermath. After stepping onto the cleansed earth, he received instructions from God that reflected his position as a covenant head tasked with guiding humanity's future. Echoing the mandate given to Adam, God commanded Noah and his sons to, *"be fruitful and multiply, and fill the earth."* (Genesis 9:1)

Yet, in this post-flood world, God also instituted a new decree:

"Whoever sheds man's blood, by man his blood shall be shed; for in the image of God He made man." (Genesis 9:6)

This establishment of justice underscored the sanctity of human life and set a foundation for order in a creation still touched by sin. Through Noah, God reestablished principles of stewardship and accountability, entrusting him with the moral framework for a reborn world.

The covenant with Noah carries profound theological weight, revealing a God who, despite humanity's sinfulness, remains devoted to His creation. The rainbow, arching across the heavens, symbolizes not just the end of wrath but the promise of redemption, a theme that weaves through Scripture. Noah's covenant foreshadows later covenants with Abraham, Moses, and David, each building toward the ultimate covenant fulfilled in Jesus Christ, the perfect covenant head who redeems all things. Noah's obedience, preserving life through the floodwaters, prefigures Christ's work, carrying humanity through the judgment of sin to eternal life. In Noah, we see a man whose faith altered history, representing all creation before God and pointing to the greater salvation yet to come.

Noah's significance as a covenant head becomes even clearer when contrasted with Adam. Adam's disobedience in Eden introduced sin and death into the world, fracturing humanity's relationship with God and subjecting creation to a curse. Noah, however, charted a different course. His steadfast obedience, laboring for decades to build the ark despite a mocking, corrupt world, brought preservation and hope where Adam's failure had brought ruin. While Adam's actions echoed through history as a legacy of loss, Noah's faithfulness rippled outward as a testament to renewal, securing life for both humanity and the animal kingdom. As covenant heads, both men shaped the destiny of those they represented, but Noah's righteousness marked a turning point, a divine reset for a fallen world.

ABRAHAM: THE FATHER OF FAITH

Abraham stands as a monumental figure in the biblical narrative, his life marking the launch of God's redemptive mission for humanity. While Noah's covenant with God brought stability to a world broken by sin, Abraham's covenant set in motion a divine plan of redemption for all nations through Jesus Christ. His story, rooted in faith and obedience, begins with a transformative call from God in Genesis 12:1-3:

> *"Get out of your country, from your family, and from your father's house, to a land that I will show you. I will make you a great nation; I will bless you and make your name great; and you shall be a blessing...and in you all the families of the earth shall be blessed."*

This wasn't just a personal promise, it established Abraham as a covenant head, a representative not only for the nation of Israel but for all who would follow in his footsteps of faith, reshaping the course of history.

The covenant between God and Abraham deepened over time, each stage reinforcing his role as its head. In Genesis 15, God reaffirmed His promise through a striking covenant ceremony. Later, in Genesis 17, God introduced circumcision as the covenant's physical sign, a mark on Abraham, his descendants, and his entire household. It symbolized their dedication to God's ways, a cutting away of their old lives, and their inclusion in the covenant's blessings and responsibilities. Through these moments, Abraham's position as a covenant head expanded, binding generations to God's redemptive purpose.

At the core of Abraham's significance lies his extraordinary faith, a trust so deep it redefined humanity's relationship with God. In Genesis 15:6, Scripture records,

"And he believed in the Lord, and He accounted it to him for right-eousness."

This pivotal moment captures Abraham's belief in God's promise of a son, despite his and Sarah's advanced age, demonstrating a faith rooted not in visible evidence but in God's unchanging character. This act established a foundational principle: righteousness comes through faith, not works. Abraham's trust didn't just secure his own standing before God; it set a pattern that would define the covenant community for centuries, influencing how future generations would approach their relationship with the divine.

Abraham's role as a covenant head carried implications far beyond his immediate family or the nation of Israel. God's promise to bless all nations through him found its ultimate fulfillment in Jesus Christ, the singular *"Seed"* of Abraham. As Paul wrote in Galatians 3:16,

"Now to Abraham and his Seed were the promises made. He does not say, 'And to seeds,' as of many, but as of one, 'And to your Seed,' who is Christ."

Through Abraham's lineage, the Messiah emerged, whose life, death, and resurrection extended the covenant's blessings to all humanity, Jew and Gentile alike. Abraham's obedience and faith thus opened the door for countless generations to enter God's redemptive plan, making him a conduit of blessing for the entire w orld.

Abraham's life offers a blueprint for understanding the role of covenant heads in God's story. His faith, tested by decades of waiting and moments of doubt, ultimately paved the way for others to experience God's promises. As a representative, his obedience shaped the destiny of those under his care, illustrating that covenant heads are active participants in God's mission, not passive figureheads. His legacy is one of hope, proving that God's plans prevail despite human weakness. Abraham's journey, from leaving his homeland to trusting in an impossible promise, shows that faith in God's word unlocks the covenant's blessings, a truth that resonates through history and culminates in Christ's redemptive work.

PHINEHAS: A PERPETUAL PRIESTHOOD

Phinehas, though often overshadowed by towering figures like Moses or David, emerges as a striking example of a covenant head whose bold resolve not only altered his own fate but secured a legacy for generations. Born into the priestly lineage of Aaron, Phinehas was the son of Eleazar and grandson of Israel's first high priest. He grew up amid a nation freshly delivered from Egypt, a people prone to both miraculous triumphs and staggering failures.

In Numbers 25, the Israelites, encamped in the plains of Moab, were on the cusp of entering the Promised Land after their exodus from Egypt. However, they succumbed to temptation, influenced by Moabite women who invited them to participate in idolatrous worship of Baal, a Canaanite deity, and engage in sexual immorality. Numbers 25:1-3 (NIV) states,

> *"While Israel was staying in Shittim, the men began to indulge in sexual immorality with Moabite women, who invited them to the sacrifices to their gods. The people ate the sacrificial meal and bowed down before these gods. So Israel yoked themselves to the Baal of Peor. And the Lord's anger burned against them."*

This was a profound betrayal of the covenant made at Sinai (Exodus 19-24), where Israel pledged to worship God alone and obey His commandments.

The covenant at Sinai was a binding agreement, uniting God and Israel in a relationship akin to a marriage, with God as their sole Lord and the Israelites as His chosen people. Central to this covenant was the command to avoid idolatry, as articulated in the first two commandments:

"You shall have no other gods before Me" and *"You shall not make for yourself a carved image."* (Exodus 20:3-4)

By worshipping Baal and engaging in the associated rituals, which often included sexual immorality, the Israelites violated the core of their covenantal relationship with God. This act of spiritual and moral infidelity provoked God's righteous anger, as their actions undermined the exclusive devotion He required.

The plague, which killed 24,000 Israelites, was a divine judgment, a consequence of their covenant violation. In the biblical worldview, God's covenants carry blessings for obedience and curses for disobedience, as outlined in Deuteronomy 28. The Sinai Covenant explicitly warned that turning to other gods would bring severe consequences, including pestilence and destruction. The plague, therefore, was not an arbitrary punishment but a fulfillment of the covenant's terms, reflecting God's justice in response to Israel's unfaithfulness. Numbers 25:3 (NIV) notes that,

"the Lord's anger burned against them,"

indicating that their idolatry and immorality directly triggered this calamity.

The narrative also suggests a broader cultural and spiritual threat. The Moabites, possibly influenced by Balaam's counsel (Numbers 31:16, Revelation 2:14), deliberately lured Israel into sin to weaken them before entering Canaan. This seduction was strategic, exploiting Israel's vulnerability to assimilate into the surrounding pagan cultures. By participating in Baal worship, the Israelites not only broke their covenant with God but also risked losing their distinct identity as His chosen people. The plague, in this sense, served as both judgment and a divine intervention to halt their spiritual decline, preserving the nation for its covenantal purpose.

The crisis reached a tipping point when an Israelite named Zimri, from the tribe of Simeon, brazenly paraded a Moabite woman, Cozbi, into the camp, flaunting their union before Moses and the assembly (Numbers 25:6). While the leaders wept in apparent paralysis, Phinehas, a priest and grandson of Aaron, took decisive action. Seizing a spear, he killed the couple, halting the plague (Numbers 25:7-8). His zealous act demonstrated unwavering loyalty to God and the covenant, restoring order and appeasing divine wrath. As a result, God declared,

> *"Phinehas son of Eleazar, the son of Aaron, the priest, has turned my anger away from the Israelites. Since he was as zealous for my honor among them as I am, I did not put an end to them in my zeal."*
> (Numbers 25:11, NIV)

God then granted Phinehas and his descendants a,

> *"covenant of a lasting priesthood,"* (Numbers 25:13)

recognizing his role as a covenant head who upheld God's honor.

His stand didn't just end a crisis; it was a pivotal act of faithfulness that rippled outward. The covenant of peace granted to Phinehas ensured that his descendants would inherit a sacred calling, serving as priests in God's presence for generations. In a moment of moral collapse, when Israel teetered on the edge of destruction, Phinehas's courage drew a line in the sand, blending justice with intercession. His legacy as a covenant head reveals a timeless truth: one person's unwavering commitment to God can shift the destiny of an entire line, turning judgment into blessing and chaos into enduring peace.

The priestly lineage of Phinehas includes several notable figures who upheld the sacred duties of the Aaronic priesthood in Israel. Zadok served as high priest under King David and King Solomon, demonstrating unwavering loyalty during Absalom's rebellion and anointing Solomon as king. Ahimaaz, Zadok's son, served as a priest under Solomon and played a key role as a messenger during Absalom's rebellion, though his specific priestly duties are less detailed. Azariah, Ahimaaz's son, was a priest likely during Solomon's reign, associated with temple service following its construction. The lineage continued through later descendants like Hilkiah, who, as high priest under Josiah, discovered the Book of the Law, sparking a national revival, and Ezra, a priest and scribe who led post-exilic reforms, teaching the law and restoring worship. These priests maintained Phinehas' covenantal legacy through their roles in worship, leadership, and spiritual reform, ensuring the continuity of Israel's covenant relationship with God.

DAVID AND GOLIATH: BATTLE OF COVENANT HEADS

David's confrontation with Goliath stands as a defining moment that vividly illustrates his role as a covenant head for Israel. This encounter was a covenantal showdown with the destiny of two nations hanging in the balance. David stepped into this role as Israel's covenant head, facing Goliath, the Philistines' representative, in a battle that would determine whether Israel would triumph or be enslaved.

The scene is charged with tension. Israel's army, gripped by fear, stood powerless as Goliath's taunts echoed daily, mocking both them and God. As David faced Goliath, he declared,

> *"You come to me with a sword, with a spear, and with a javelin. But I come to you in the name of the Lord of hosts, the God of the armies of Israel, whom you have defied."* (1 Samuel 17:45)

In that moment, David's faith and actions represented all of Israel, binding their fate to his stand against the giant.

When David's stone struck Goliath's forehead, felling the giant with a single blow, the victory rippled far beyond a personal triumph. The Philistines fled, and Israel pursued, securing a decisive win. This was not David's victory alone; it was Israel's deliverance, won through their covenant head. Had David fallen, the nation would have faced servitude, but because he prevailed, all Israel reaped the reward of freedom. His faith and courage in this pivotal moment determined the destiny of many under his representation, showcasing the profound influence of a covenant head. By standing firm against Goliath, David's obedience and trust in God brought liberation and renewed hope to his people, altering the course of their history. This triumph offers a glimpse into the power of a covenant head to shape the future, pointing toward a greater head whose victory would resonate eternally.

The theological weight of this battle extends even further, pointing to Christ, the ultimate covenant head. David's triumph over Goliath foreshadows Jesus' victory over sin and death, a parallel that Paul unpacks in Romans 5:18-19:

> *"Therefore, as through one man's offense judgment came to all men, resulting in condemnation, even so through one Man's righteous act the free gift came to all men, resulting in justification of life. For as by one man's disobedience many were made sinners, so also by one Man's obedience many will be made righteous."*

Just as David's success liberated Israel from Philistine oppression, Christ's resurrection frees humanity from the bondage of sin, fulfilling the role of the perfect covenant head. David's temporal victory serves as a shadow of this eternal redemption, linking his story to the broader narrative of God's salvation plan.

Moreover, this event underscores the communal nature of covenant relationships. In ancient Israel, the actions of a leader like David had profound implications for the entire community. His faith and courage were not just personal attributes; they were blessings that uplifted all Israel. When David triumphed, the victory belonged to the nation, reinforcing their covenant bond with God. This interconnectedness highlights a core truth of covenant theology: the head and the people are united, their fates intertwined. David's stand against Goliath thus becomes a powerful illustration of how one person's faithfulness can shift the tide for many, echoing through Israel's history and pointing toward the ultimate covenant head, Christ, whose obedience secures redemption for all who are in H im.

DAVID AND JONATHAN: BROTHERLY LOVE

Now we shift to a quieter, yet equally profound moment: the covenant between David and Jonathan. After David's triumph over Goliath, he and Jonathan, King Saul's son, forged a covenant of profound loyalty as Jonathan recognized God's favor upon David. In 1 Samuel 18:1-3, we read:

> *"The soul of Jonathan was knit to the soul of David, and Jonathan loved him as his own soul. Saul took him that day, and would not let him go home to his father's house anymore. Then Jonathan and David made a covenant, because he loved him as his own soul."*

At this point, Saul initially favors David (1 Samuel 18:5), appointing him over his men and welcoming his success. However, Saul becomes envious of David's popularity after the people praise David more than Saul. Saul's jealousy consumed him, his bitterness spreads like a disease through the palace, contaminating servants and family members alike, poisoning his household against David (1 Samuel 18:8-9). Yet Jonathan stood apart. His heart remained unbound by that hatred. He recognized and honored God's hand upon David's life and chose covenant love over family loyalty, a bond thicker than blood ties. The contrast between father and son could not be starker. This jealousy escalates, and by 1 Samuel 19:1, Saul explicitly orders his servants and Jonathan to kill David. The covenant between David and Jonathan transcends the natural order of loyalty to family. Though Jonathan is heir to Saul's throne, he acknowledges God's choice of David as the next king.

Jonathan's soul became knit to David's soul, establishing a covenant relationship that would define both their lives and surpass ordinary human affection. Their love, as David later mourns in 2 Samuel 1:26, was,

> *"wonderful, surpassing the love of women."*

Some twist this into a romantic lens as a homosexual relationship, revealing a fundamental misunderstanding of biblical covenant language. This was covenantal love that exemplified a spiritual connection that operated on a higher plane than physical or romantic love. The strength of their covenant would be tested through years of trials as Saul pursued David's life. Jonathan remained steadfast in his covenant loyalty, even when it meant standing against his own father's murderous intentions.

According to the customs of covenant-making, when they cut their covenant, all of David's family existed within him as covenant head, and all of Jonathan's family existed within him. This meant that the covenant benefits and obligations would pass down to their descendants, even those yet unborn. This promise bears fruit after tragedy strikes. In 1 Samuel 31, Jonathan died alongside Saul and his brothers in battle against the Philistines. Upon hearing the news, David's lament over Jonathan's death revealed the depth of their covenant bond. This grief surpassed mourning a fallen comrade; David anguished over losing his covenant brother, whose life was a sacred covenant supernaturally bound to his own.

Years later, as king, David recalled his covenant, asking,

> *"Is there still anyone who is left of the house of Saul, that I may show him kindness for Jonathan's sake?"* (2 Samuel 9:1)

That phrase, *"for Jonathan's sake,"* is the heartbeat of the story. It's not about the recipient's merit, but the covenant's enduring power. A servant revealed that Jonathan's son, Mephibosheth, lived, crippled in both feet from a childhood accident when his nurse dropped him fleeing Saul's downfall (2 Samuel 4:4). Raised in Lo-debar, a barren "middle of nowhere", Mephibosheth grew up on lies that David had stole his throne and would kill him. When David summoned him, he arrived trembling, expecting death. Instead, David spoke grace:

"Do not fear, for I will surely show you kindness for Jonathan your father's sake, and will restore to you all the land of Saul your grandfather, and you shall eat at my table continually." (2 Samuel 9:7)

Mephibosheth, overwhelmed, replied,

"What is your servant, that you should look upon such a dead dog as I?" (2 Samuel 9:8)

Shame and unworthiness gripped him, yet David brushed it aside, granting him a place at the king's table as a son.

Mephibosheth didn't earn this; he received it because he was "in Jonathan" when the covenant was made. His lameness, those broken legs, didn't disqualify him. Under the table, no one saw his weakness; he dined as royalty because of his father's bond with David. This story mirrors our own, hinting at a greater covenant head whose faithfulness secured our place.

JESUS: THE ULTIMATE COVENANT HEAD

Throughout the Bible, figures like Adam, Noah, Abraham, David, and Jonathan each served as covenant heads, their lives pointing forward to the One in whom all promises find fulfillment: Jesus Christ. As the ultimate covenant head, Jesus not only completed the story begun by these earlier figures but also transforms it, securing eternal life and righteousness for all who are united to Him through faith .

Adam, the first man, stood as humanity's representative in Eden. His disobedience shattered our communion with God, unleashing sin and death like a flood across the earth. Every person born bears the mark of his fall, a cracked vessel unable to hold the fullness of divine life. Yet, Jesus steps into history as the second Adam and reversed the curse. When He hung on the cross, scars marking His hands, feet, and side, He wasn't just a victim; He was our representative, our covenant head. His perfect obedience and sacrificial death paid the debt we could not, sealing a new covenant with His blood and restoring what Adam lost.

This new covenant stands apart from those that came before. Unlike the covenant with Adam, which hinged on human faithfulness and crumbled under our frailty, and unlike the Mosaic covenant, which exposed our inability to keep God's law, the new covenant is an unbreakable pact between God the Father and God the Son. Hebrews 7:22 declares,

> *"By so much more Jesus has become a surety of a better covenant."*

Jesus Himself guarantees its success, His eternal priesthood ensuring that it cannot fail. Through faith, we are grafted into Him, as Galatians 3:29 affirms:

> *"And if you are Christ's, then you are Abraham's seed, and heirs according to the promise."*

Jesus, the singular seed of Abraham (Galatians 3:16), fulfills every covenant promise, from the rainbow of Noah to the throne of David, making us co-heirs of a blessing we could never earn. In Him, the scattered threads of God's covenants are woven into a tapestry of grace.

Like Mephibosheth, we don't earn our seat at the King's table; we receive it "for Jesus' sake." Our legs remain broken by the fall. Our spiritual lameness, sin and weakness, remains, yet at God's table, it is hidden beneath the grace of our covenant head. We sit as sons and daughters, clothed in His righteousness. Galatians 3:28 proclaims this unity,

> *"There is neither Jew nor Greek, there is neither slave nor free, there is neither male nor female; for you are all one in Christ Jesus."*

In Him, our broken identities are remade, our guilt is covered, and our inheritance is secured.

Jesus' role as covenant head is the heartbeat of the gospel. Where Adam's sin condemned us, Christ's obedience justifies us. Where the law revealed our failure, His blood cleanses us. Where death once reigned, His resurrection brings life. This new covenant rests not on our faltering efforts, but on His finished work. As our representative, Jesus has fulfilled every demand, defeated every foe, and won every blessing. Understanding this truth is vital to unlocking the secret of the lord. We are invited to rest in Him, to trust in His victory, and to live as heirs of an eternal promise, a promise sealed by the scars of our ultimate covenant head. In Jesus, the covenant story reaches its glorious climax, drawing us into a relationship with God that cannot be broken, where grace abounds and love endures forever.

LIVING AS COVENANT HEIRS

If Jesus is our covenant head, what's our role? Does His work erase our responsibility? Not at all. First, it shifts our posture from earning to receiving. Mephibosheth overcame his unworthiness by trusting David's kindness; we must trust Christ's. Our salvation rests not on our holiness, but on His, credited to us as our head. This frees us to approach God boldly, knowing our brokenness doesn't bar us from His table.

Second, it redefines our identity. We're not lone wanderers; we're the Israel of God (Galatians 6:16), united under Christ, heirs to Abraham's promises through faith. This communal bond calls us to love and defend one another, as covenant siblings should.

Finally, it anchors our confidence. In a world of shifting loyalties, Jesus stands unwavering. His scars, those eternal reminders, assure us that our covenant is secure. No giant, no lie, no failure can sever what He's sealed. Like David facing Goliath, we can confront life's challenges, knowing our head has already won.

Covenant heads are God's chosen vessels to weave us into His story. From Adam's stumble to Jesus' triumph, they shape our destiny, binding us to God's faithfulness. David's sling felled a giant for Israel; Jonathan's love lifted Mephibosheth from exile; Christ's cross redeems us from sin's curse. Through faith, we inherit their legacy, not by our merit, but by their representation. So lift your eyes from Lo-debar's dust. You're not a cripple in hiding; you're a child at the King's table, welcomed by the blood of your covenant head. Fear Him, trust Him, and let His secret transform you.

CHAPTER 7

COVENANT EXCHANGES

C ovenant bonds were often sealed through specific rituals and exchanges that carried deep symbolic weight, transforming the participants and their communities. Among these customs, the exchange of names, belts or girdles, and garments stands out as powerful expressions of the covenant relationship. These acts were tangible demonstrations of mutual identification, commitment, and shared identity. In this chapter, we will explore these three key covenant exchanges, drawing from Scripture and cultural insights to uncover their meaning and significance. We'll see how they illuminate our relationship with God, particularly through the New Covenant established by Jesus Christ, and how they remain relevant to us today.

RITUAL 5 – THE EXCHANGE OF NAMES

The fifth custom of biblical covenants centers on the exchange of names between covenant partners. Names in the ancient world were not just labels; they carried a person's essence, character, and destiny. To exchange names in a covenant was to share one's identity with another, declaring a unity that transcended individuality. In Scripture, this practice is vividly illustrated when God enters covenant with His people, often marking the occasion with a new name that reflects their transformed relationship.

Consider Abraham, originally named Abram, which means "exalted father." In Genesis 17:5, God declared,

> *"No longer shall your name be called Abram, but your name shall*
> *be Abraham; for I have made you a father of many nations."*

This renaming occurs as God reaffirms His covenant with Abraham, promising him descendants as numerous as the stars. The new name, Abraham, incorporates a breathy "H" sound, which some scholars suggest echoes the divine name of God (often represented as YHWH or "Yahweh," pronounced with an aspirated "H"). Similarly, Sarai becomes Sarah, meaning "princess," signifying her role as the mother of nations (Genesis 17:15-16). These changes proclaim a new identity tied to God's promise and presence.

Another striking example is Jacob, whose name means "supplanter" or "deceiver," reflecting his early life of cunning. In Genesis 32:28, after wrestling with God, he is renamed Israel, meaning "he struggles with God" or "prince of God." This new name marks a pivotal shift, aligning his identity with his covenant relationship with God and his role as the father of the twelve tribes. In the New Testament, we see this pattern continue with Simon, whom Jesus renames Peter, meaning "rock," signifying his foundational role in the church (Matthew 16:18), and Saul, who becomes Paul, reflecting his mission to the Gentiles (Acts 13:9).

In covenant terms, exchanging names is a declaration of mutual belonging: "I am now part of you, and you are part of me." It's a profound act of identification, where the parties' fates become intertwined. When God exchanges names with His people, He is no longer just "God" in the abstract; He becomes,

> *"the God of Abraham, the God of Isaac, and the God of Jacob,"*
> (Exodus 3:6)

and ultimately, "my God" to each believer. This personal connection is emphasized in the New Covenant, where we are called, *"children of God,"* (John 1:12)

and God becomes,

"our Father." (Matthew 6:9)

Revelation 2:17 promises that those who overcome will receive,

"a white stone, and on the stone a new name written which no one knows except him who receives it,"

suggesting a deeply personal identity bestowed by God.

This exchange also grants authority. In ancient covenants, taking another's name often meant wielding their power or acting on their behalf. When Jesus instructs His disciples to pray and act,

"in My name," (John 14:13-14)

He's giving them a covenantal privilege. Colossians 3:17 says,

"And whatever you do in word or deed, do all in the name of the Lord Jesus, giving thanks to God the Father through Him."

God wants us to live in the authority and identity of Christ, rooted in our covenant with Him. Every prayer in the New Testament, though not always ending with "in Jesus' name," is offered in His authority, reflecting this covenantal reality.

Mark 16:17-18 (ESV) recorded Jesus saying,

"And these signs will accompany those who believe: in my name they will cast out demons; they will speak in new tongues; they will pick up serpents with their hands; and if they drink any deadly poison, it will not hurt them; they will lay their hands on the sick, and they will recover."

This authority to preach, heal, and cast out demons "in His name" empowered the disciples to act as His representatives, carrying His presence and power into the world.

This authority permeates every aspect of life. Whether praying for provision, confronting evil, or sharing the good news, acting "in Jesus' name" means operating under His delegated power. It's akin to an ambassador speaking with the king's authority, when aligned with Christ's will, believers carry the full weight of His name, making their words and actions effective because of the covenant that undergirds them.

This has everything to do with your revelation and understanding of covenant. Without grasping the depth of what it means to be in covenant with God through Jesus, we risk reducing "in Jesus' name" to a religious catchphrase, hoping it magically enhances our prayers or deeds. But the true power lies in understanding the covenant itself. Jesus' blood sealed this bond, uniting us with Him and granting us His name as a sign of authority. Revelation of this covenant transforms how we live. It's not about what we say, but who we are in Him. When we comprehend that we are covenant partners with God, we approach life with boldness, knowing our identity and authority stem from Christ's finished work.

In His authority, in accordance with the blood and the covenant I have, I receive whatever is rightfully mine, and I can bind anything that comes against the divine will of God. This is the practical outworking of covenantal authority. Through Jesus, we have access to God's promises—provision, protection, healing, and victory—because they are our inheritance as covenant children (John 1:12). When we pray or act in His name, aligned with His will, we can confidently receive what He has promised. Simultaneously, we have the authority to "bind" anything opposing God's divine will, be it sickness, oppression, or spiritual attack. Matthew 18:18 reinforces this:

> *"Assuredly, I say to you, whatever you bind on earth will be bound in heaven, and whatever you loose on earth will be loosed in heaven."*

We don't have any power on our own, it's the covenantal right granted through Christ's sacrifice and activated by our faith in the covenant.

The exchange of names finds a human parallel in marriage, where the wife takes her husband's surname, symbolizing unity and shared authority. This practice mirrors our covenant with God and offers a tangible picture of its intimacy and power. In marriage, a wife gains access to her husband's resources, name, and authority within the family, much like believers gain access to God's promises through Christ. When a woman takes her husband's name, it's a public declaration of belonging, she is now part of his household, and he is committed to her. Similarly, as Christians, we bear Christ's name, marking us as part of God's family and sharers in His authority.

Marriage reflects the divine union between Christ and the church, as Paul wrote in Ephesians 5:25-32:

> *"Husbands, love your wives, just as Christ loved the church and gave Himself up for her...This is a great mystery, but I speak concerning Christ and the church."*

In this covenant, two become one, sharing not just their lives but their identities. The exchange of names in marriage signifies a transfer of loyalty and allegiance, the wife leaves her father's house to join her husband's, just as we leave our old life to embrace our new identity in Christ (2 Corinthians 5:17). It's a mutual commitment: the husband pledges to provide, protect, and cherish, while the wife commits to support and honor. Likewise, God promises to be our provider, protector, and guide, and we vow to love, obey, and serve Him. Marriage thus illuminates our covenant with Christ, where the exchange of names unites us in love, loyalty, and authority, reflecting the eternal bond we share with Him.

RITUAL 6 – THE EXCHANGE OF BELTS OR GIRDLES

The sixth custom of biblical covenants involves the sacred exchange of belts or girdles between covenant partners. In biblical times, the belt or girdle was a practical item that held weapons, like swords or daggers, symbolizing strength and readiness for battle. To exchange belts in a covenant ceremony was to pledge mutual protection and defense, a commitment to stand together against any threat. This act declared, "Your enemies are my enemies, and I will fight for you," cementing a bond of loyalty and support.

In 1 Samuel 18:1-4, after David's victory over Goliath, he and Jonathan, King Saul's son, form a profound covenant of friendship. Jonathan seals this bond by giving David his robe, tunic, sword, bow, and belt, symbolizing his pledge to protect and support David. This act carries deep significance, as Jonathan entrusts David with his weapons. The covenant is established before King Saul's jealousy emerges, which later leads him to seek David's life (1 Samuel 18:6-11; 19:1). Despite Saul's growing hostility, Jonathan's loyalty to David surpasses his familial ties, showcasing the depth of their covenantal commitment.

In Ruth 1:16, though not explicitly an exchange of belts, we see a similar spirit of mutual support when Ruth pledges to Naomi,

> *"For wherever you go, I will go; And wherever you lodge, I will lodge;*
> *Your people shall be my people, And your God, my God."*

This commitment reflects the protective bond inherent in covenant relationships, where one party's welfare becomes the other's responsibility.

In God's covenant with humanity, this exchange takes on divine dimensions. In Genesis 15:1, God told Abraham,

"Do not be afraid, Abram. I am your shield, your exceedingly great reward."

Here, God positions Himself as Abram's protector, offering His strength in place of Abram's vulnerability. This promise is echoed in Psalm 91:4,

"He shall cover you with His feathers, And under His wings you shall take refuge; His truth shall be your shield and buckler."

In the New Covenant, this protection is extended through the,

"armor of God,"

described in Ephesians 6:10-18, which includes the,

"belt of truth."

By equipping us with His armor, God pledges to defend us against spiritual enemies, ensuring our safety in the battles of life.

Conversely, as covenant partners, we are called to stand for God. This doesn't mean physical warfare but a commitment to uphold His truth and kingdom purposes. In 2 Timothy 2:3-4, Paul urged believers to endure hardship,

"as a good soldier of Jesus Christ,"

reflecting our role in this mutual exchange. God's promise to protect us is met with our pledge to align with Him, creating a reciprocal bond of defense and loyalty.

To give a more recent story of covenant exchanges, you may have heard of two remarkable men in the 1800s who ventured into the heart of Africa, bringing with them not just exploration and missionary work, but a profound understanding of covenant relationships that would transform entire tribes. Henry Morton Stanley and David Livingston discovered that the concept of covenant resonated deeply with African tribal cultures.

Livingston, in particular, found extraordinary success in sharing the Gospel by presenting it through the lens of covenant relationships. As he ventured into the deepest regions of Africa's jungles, he encountered tribes who, despite their isolation from Western civilization, held a deep understanding of covenant bonds. Rather than attempting to impose foreign concepts, Livingston leveraged their existing knowledge of blood covenants to explain God's relationship with humanity.

One of the most striking examples of covenant relationships Livingston encountered was between the Watusi and Pygmy tribes. These two groups, despite their vast physical differences—the Watusi being remarkably tall and the Pygmies being of small stature—had established a powerful covenant bond. This covenant meant that if anyone attempted to harm a Pygmy, they would face the full might of the Watusi warriors, as the covenant made them one people.

The Watusi, known for their impressive height and warrior culture, had entered this protective covenant with the Pygmies primarily to provide defense. Through this covenant relationship, the Pygmies gained the protection of some of Africa's most formidable warriors. If anyone dared to attack or mistreat a Pygmy, they would face the same response as if they had attacked a Watusi, for in covenant, an attack on one partner was considered an attack on both.

Their experiences among African tribes revealed that covenant concepts transcended cultural boundaries. The universal understanding of covenant bonds among these tribes demonstrated that God had embedded these principles deep within human consciousness, preparing the way for people to understand His covenant relationship with humanity through Christ. Many Christians today fail to recognize their covenant relationship with God and fellow believers. If we truly grasped that God is our shield, and we are His people, it would reshape our interactions, ending gossip and division, and fostering a community that defends and uplifts each other. If believers truly understood this covenant bond, it would revolutionize their relationships within the church.

RITUAL 7 – THE EXCHANGE OF GARMENTS

The seventh custom of biblical covenants centered on the exchange of garments between covenant partners. Throughout history, across diverse cultures spanning thousands of years, clothing has served as a powerful symbol of one's social position and possessions. In ancient societies, people recognized individuals' status and position by their clothing. A priest's garments distinguished them from others. A warrior's attire marked their role. A king's robes declared their authority. Even today, this principle continues; police officers are recognized by their uniforms, doctors by their white coats, and firefighters by their distinctive gear.

Garments in Scripture often represent identity, status, or spiritual condition. From Adam and Eve's fig leaves replaced by God's provision of skins (Genesis 3:21) to Joseph's coat of many colors signifying favor (Genesis 37:3), clothing carries symbolic weight. In a covenant, exchanging garments means sharing one's identity and resources, declaring, what's mine is yours, and what's yours is mine. This act signifies a complete union where status and possessions are held in common, forging a bond of mutual commitment and trust.

Jonathan's gift of his robe to David (1 Samuel 18:4) exemplifies this custom, carrying profound significance within the context of their covenant relationship. Jonathan, the prince with a kingdom to inherit, and David, the shepherd anointed as God's chosen king. When Jonathan gives David his robe, he symbolically shares his royal authority and privilege, aligning himself with David's destiny over his own birthright. This act signifies a surrender of personal ambition, as Jonathan recognizes David as God's appointed leader. The robe, a visible emblem of his princely rank, becomes a tangible declaration of their unity, a commitment that Jonathan will stand with David. This exchange deepens their covenant, intertwining their identities and fates in a way that foreshadows the self-giving love of the New Covenant.

Similarly, when Elijah casts his cloak over Elisha in 1 Kings 19:19, it marks the transfer of prophetic authority, inviting Elisha into a covenantal relationship that binds their lives and ministries together in a profound partnership. At this moment, Elijah, the seasoned prophet of Israel, is directed by God (1 Kings 19:16) to anoint Elisha as his successor, a divine call that begins with this symbolic act. The cloak, worn and weathered from Elijah's years of confronting kings and speaking God's word, represents his prophetic office, his authority, and his identity as God's mouthpiece. By throwing it over Elisha, a farmer plowing his fields, Elijah initiates a covenant bond, calling Elisha to share in his mission and destiny.

Elisha's response, leaving his oxen, burning his plow, and following Elijah (1 Kings 19:20-21), demonstrates his full commitment to this covenant, a surrender of his former life to embrace a shared journey with Elijah. Their relationship grows into one of mentorship and mutual reliance, as seen later in 2 Kings 2:1-14, where Elisha remains steadfastly by Elijah's side until the moment Elijah is taken up to heaven. As they walk and talk together, a chariot of fire and horses of fire appear, separating them, and Elijah ascends in a whirlwind (2 Kings 2:11), marking his extraordinary departure from earth without experiencing death. When Elisha picks up Elijah's fallen cloak after his ascent and uses it to part the Jordan River (2 Kings 2:13-14), the garment exchange is completed, signifying that Elijah's authority and spirit now rest on Elisha. This covenant, forged through the cloak, unites them across time, Elijah as the forerunner and Elisha as the inheritor, reflecting a bond of loyalty, purpose, and divine commissioning that echoes the New Covenant's promise of shared inheritance and empowerment.

The High Priest's Garments (Exodus 28:1-43) offer a compelling example of a covenantal exchange, as God instructs Moses to craft elaborate garments for Aaron, his brother, to wear as the high priest ministering before the Lord. These garments—including the ephod, breastplate, robe, tunic, turban, and sash—are meticulously designed with gold, blue, purple, and scarlet threads, adorned with precious stones and bells, reflecting their sacred purpose.

God commands Moses in Exodus 28:2 to make these,

"holy garments for Aaron your brother, for glory and for beauty,"

signifying Aaron's consecrated role as the mediator between God and Israel. This act is a covenantal transfer, as Moses, the leader and prophet chosen to deliver God's law, invests Aaron with the authority and identity of the priesthood, binding them together in service to God's covenant with His people. Their relationship, rooted in brotherhood and divine calling, is deepened by this exchange: Moses, who speaks face-to-face with God (Exodus 33:11), equips Aaron to enter the Holy of Holies on behalf of the nation, a role Aaron could not assume without Moses' mediation and God's instruction.

The breastplate, bearing the names of the twelve tribes (Exodus 28:29), symbolizes Aaron carrying Israel's burdens before God, while the Urim and Thummim within it (Exodus 28:30) signify his access to divine guidance, privileges bestowed through this covenantal act. Leviticus 8:7-9 further details Moses dressing Aaron in these garments during his consecration, a hands-on ritual that seals their partnership in fulfilling the covenant established at Sinai (Exodus 19:5-6). The intricate design and sacred purpose of these clothes highlight how garments represent authority and divine appointment, uniting Moses and Aaron in a shared mission to lead, intercede, and uphold God's relationship with Israel, prefiguring the New Covenant where all believers are clothed as priests (1 Peter 2:9).

Ruth and Boaz (Ruth 3:9, NIV) provide a poignant illustration of a covenantal garment exchange, rooted in a moment of vulnerability and trust that blossoms into a profound partnership. In this scene, Ruth, a widowed Moabite, approaches Boaz at the threshing floor under Naomi's guidance, lying at his feet and asking him to,

"spread the corner of your garment over me, since you are a guardian-redeemer of our family."

This request, often translated as "spread your wing," is a symbolic plea for protection and redemption, invoking the custom of a kinsman-redeemer under Mosaic law (Leviticus 25:25).

Boaz, a wealthy landowner and relative of Naomi's deceased husband, responds with compassion and honor, affirming in Ruth 3:10-11 his willingness to act as her redeemer. By agreeing to cover her with his garment, Boaz signifies his commitment to take Ruth under his care, redeem her family's land, and marry her, establishing a new covenantal bond that transcends their initial social divide—Ruth as a foreigner and Boaz as an Israelite of standing.

This exchange is not a literal handing over of a cloak but a powerful metaphor enacted through his promise, as seen in Ruth 4:9-10, where Boaz publicly declares his intent to redeem Naomi's property and take Ruth as his wife before the elders at the gate. Their covenant is further sealed by God's blessing, as Ruth becomes the mother of Obed, grandfather to King David, placing her in the lineage of Christ (Ruth 4:17, Matthew 1:5). Ruth's bold request reflects her faith in Boaz's character, while his response embodies the care, provision, and unity central to covenant partnerships. This act of "covering" mirrors God's protective love over His people (Ezekiel 16:8), foreshadowing the New Covenant where Christ redeems and unites believers into His family.

In the New Covenant, the exchange of garments reaches its ultimate expression. Galatians 3:27 (NIV) declares,

> *"For all of you who were baptized into Christ have clothed yourselves with Christ."*

To be *"clothed with Christ"* is to take on His identity and righteousness, a divine exchange where Jesus takes our sin and gives us His purity (2 Corinthians 5:21). This is not a metaphor but a covenant reality that transforms how God perceives us. When we stand before Him, He sees His Son's righteousness, not our shortcomings. Revelation 3:5 promises that overcomers will be, *"clothed in white,"*

symbolizing victory and purity, a future fulfillment of this exchange.

This sharing of garments extends to inheritance. Romans 8:17 proclaims believers as,

"heirs of God and joint heirs with Christ,"

meaning we partake in all that belongs to Jesus—His authority, victory, and relationship with the Father. In Acts 2:44, the early church embodied this principle, holding,

"all things in common."

This wasn't socialism but covenant living, where unity mirrored the mutual sharing of a garment exchange. When one prospered, all rejoiced; when one suffered, all bore the burden. For believers, being clothed with Christ means our identity is secure, our resources are His, and our community reflects His oneness.

THE HEART OF COVENANT

The covenant exchanges of names, belts, and garments represent profound acts that go far beyond simple rituals, encapsulating the sharing of identity, strength, and resources between two parties. These ancient practices illustrate the depth of commitment inherent in covenant relationships, forging bonds that unite individuals in purpose and destiny. The exchange of names signifies a mutual identification, where each party adopts the essence and future of the other, creating a shared identity that transcends individuality. The exchange of belts, or girdles, symbolizes a pledge of strength and protection, a solemn vow to stand in defense and support of one another. Meanwhile, the exchange of garments reflects a generous sharing of status and resources, declaring unity and mutual provision.

Together, these exchanges combine loyalty, trust, and interdependence, revealing the heart of what it means to enter into a covenant.

These rituals find their ultimate expression and fulfillment in the New Covenant established through Jesus Christ, transforming our relationship with God in ways that are both intimate and eternal. Through His sacrifice, the exchange of names becomes a divine reality as we are renamed as children of God, adopted into His family with a new identity rooted in His unchanging love and grace. The exchange of belts takes on profound meaning as God promises to be our shield and protector, equipping us with His strength and calling us to stand boldly for His truth and kingdom purposes. The exchange of garments reaches its pinnacle as we are clothed in the righteousness of Christ—our sins exchanged for His purity—making us joint heirs with Him in His authority and inheritance. This New Covenant not only reconciles us to God but also empowers us to live as His ambassadors, reflecting His character and glory to the world.

The significance of these covenant exchanges extends beyond our personal relationship with God, shaping how we engage with others in our communities and beyond. Embracing our new identity in Christ compels us to foster unity and love, mirroring His heart in every interaction and building bridges where division once stood. The pledge of strength and protection calls us to stand alongside our brothers and sisters, advocating for justice and defending the vulnerable with the same steadfastness God shows us. Likewise, the sharing of resources challenges us to live with open hands, recognizing that all we possess is a gift from God meant to bless others and advance His kingdom. By living out these principles of unity, loyalty, and generosity, we become living testimonies of the New Covenant—vessels of hope, healing, and reconciliation in a world desperately in need of God's transformative love.

CHAPTER 8

SEALING THE COVENANT

Throughout our exploration of covenant living, we've uncovered its profound narrative: from the secret of the Lord revealed to those who revere Him, to its transformative power in the lives of Moses, David, and others. We've defined covenant as a blood bond of unwavering faithfulness, marveled at the vivid symbols, like the cutting of animals, that marked its formation, and seen how covenant heads carried promises for generations yet unborn. We've explored the intimate exchanges of names, belts, and garments that deepened the unity between partners.

But how does a promise transcend the fragility of human words, enduring through generations in a world where vows often dissolve like breath in the wind? For the those in the ancient world, it took more than a fleeting handshake or a scribbled signature, it demanded rituals that anchored the promise deep within their lives. These acts—proclaiming the terms aloud, creating a permanent landscape marker, and sharing a meal to bind hearts in trust—transformed agreements into living bonds, etched into hearts and landscapes for all time.

In this chapter, we'll immerse ourselves in these sealing rituals, drawing from Scripture to witness their unfolding in ancient covenants and reflecting on their significance. We'll discover how these acts resonate in our lives today under the New Covenant, sealed by the blood of Christ, a covenant that invites us into an eternal relationship with God. These customs reveal a God who not only commits Himself to us but ensures that His promises remain unshakable, visible, and life-giving, calling us to live as His covenant people across all generations.

RITUAL 8 – READING THE TERMS

Picture yourself standing at the base of a rugged mountain, the air humming with a strange stillness. The dust of Egypt still clings to your sandals, a faint memory of chains broken and a sea parted. Before you, Moses stands, his weathered hands clutching the words of God, his voice cutting through the silence like a blade. He speaks of promises that lift your spirit and warnings that chill your bones. This is the eighth custom of covenant-making: the reading of the terms, a public declaration that left no shadow of doubt. This act pulsed at the heart of accountability. Both parties heard their duties and rewards, the stakes laid bare in blessings and curses.

For Israel, this moment ignited at Sinai, captured vividly in Deuteronomy 28. Moses stood before the people, a nation freshly redeemed from Egypt's chains, and laid out the terms of their sacred agreement with God. He began with a vision of abundance:

> *"If you fully obey the Lord your God and carefully follow all his commands I give you today, the Lord your God will set you high above all the nations on earth. All these blessings will come on you and accompany you if you obey the Lord your God: You will be blessed in the city and blessed in the country. The fruit of your womb will be blessed, and the crops of your land and the young of your livestock—the calves of your herds and the lambs of your flocks. Your basket and your kneading trough will be blessed. You will be blessed when you come in and blessed when you go out."* (Deuteronomy 28:1-6, NIV)

The promises poured forth like a river in flood—prosperity, protection, and divine favor cascading over a people who walked in step with their Maker. It was a vision of life as it was meant to be, a harmony between God and His own, where faithfulness bore fruit in abundance. But Moses didn't stop there. The terms of a covenant are two-sided, and so he pivoted to the consequences of disobedience:

> *"However, if you do not obey the Lord your God and do not carefully follow all his commands and decrees I am giving you today, all these curses will come on you and overtake you: You will be cursed in the city and cursed in the country. Your basket and your kneading trough will be cursed. The fruit of your womb will be cursed, and the crops of your land, and the calves of your herds and the lambs of your flocks. You will be cursed when you come in and cursed when you go out."*
> (Deuteronomy 28:15-19, NIV)

The list unfurls with sobering detail—disease, drought, defeat, and exile loom as shadows over a nation that turns from its God. These were the natural outworking of a broken relationship, a mirror reflecting the gravity of rejecting the One who had delivered them.

This reading of the terms wasn't a private whisper between God and Moses, it was a communal event, proclaimed aloud so every Israelite, from gray-haired elder to wide-eyed child, could hear and understand. It echoed the ancient custom where covenant partners stood before witnesses, reciting their obligations to ensure mutual clarity. In Deuteronomy 31:10-13, Moses instructs the priests to read the Law every seven years during the Feast of Tabernacles so,

> *"that they may hear and that they may learn to fear the Lord your God and carefully observe all the words of this law."*

The repetition reinforced the covenant's terms, keeping them alive in the collective memory of a people prone to forgetfulness.

This wasn't just Israel's story. Across the ancient Near East, treaties between kings or clans often hinged on a public reading, sometimes etched onto clay or stone for the ages. Today, we see shadows of this in our own contracts, business deals spell out deliverables and penalties or a mortgage warns of foreclosure if payments falter. The principle endures: clarity forges commitment. When two companies merge, their agreement details what each must bring and what's lost if they fail, perhaps a fine or a forfeit. So too with Israel: God's terms weren't a cage but a compass, guiding them to thrive under His care. The blessings promised abundance; the curses guarded against chaos. This duality unveils God's heart, His holiness demands justice, yet His love offers a path to life. Moses later urged:

> "See, I set before you today life and prosperity, death and destruction... Now choose life, so that you and your children may live." (Deuteronomy 30:15, 19, NIV)

What does this mean for us under the New Covenant? Unlike the Sinai Covenant, where the terms hinged on Israel's obedience, a standard that would cause any of us to stumble, our bond with God rests securely on Christ's perfect faithfulness. At Sinai, Israel's obedience was the key to inheriting the land and its blessings. In Christ, His obedience unlocks a grace we could never earn through our own efforts. Hebrews 8:10-12 (NIV) beautifully unveils the New Covenant's terms: God promised to write His laws on our hearts so that all will know Him intimately from the least to the greatest, and He declared,

> "I will forgive their wickedness, and will remember their sins no more."

These aren't burdensome tasks we must labor to fulfill but precious treasures we receive by faith, transforming our inner being and securing our forgiveness.

Yet, these terms still hold profound importance for every believer. There are always terms that come with any covenant. Consider how many Christians today are born-again, entering into a profound relationship with God, yet remain unaware that they have a covenant with Him or what its terms entail. If you don't know the terms of the covenant God has made with you, how can you ever know the secret of the Lord? How can you fully embrace the promises that shape this divine relationship?

Christians must know the terms of the covenant as under the New Covenant. Jesus warns of judgment for those who spurn this grace,

> *"Whoever believes in the Son has eternal life; whoever does not obey the Son shall not see life, but the wrath of God remains on him."* (John 3:36, NIV)

Paul urges us to,

> *"work out your salvation with fear and trembling."* (Philippians 2:12, NIV)

Not to secure it through our own merit, but to live it boldly, allowing God's work in us to bear fruit. Too many drift through faith blind to these promises, missing the anchor of what God asks in return: our trust and our love.

The reading of the terms sealed the covenant by anchoring it in mutual understanding. For Israel, it was a solemn moment of commitment; for us, it's an invitation to know the God who binds Himself to us, not with chains of obligation, but with cords of love.

RITUAL 9 – TREES AND STONES AS MEMORIALS

The ninth custom of covenant-making was the establishment of a natural marker, whether a tree planted to grow and flourish or rocks piled to stand firm, serving as a living or enduring testament to the agreement. In a culture where scars marked the flesh of covenant partners, as we saw in earlier chapters, those marks faded with death. A chief might bear a scar from a covenant cut, a visible sign to his tribe of their bond with another people, but when he died, that scar went to the grave. The tree or the heap of rocks, however, endured. A tree grew, stretched its branches toward the sky, and bore fruit long after the original partners had passed, while rocks stood unmoved, their steadfast presence a silent witness. Both whispered to each new generation the story of the commitment made in their name, embedding the covenant in the landscape i tself.

ABRAHAM AND ABIMELECH

Scripture offers glimpses of covenant-making practices, sometimes explicitly, sometimes subtly woven into the narrative. In Genesis 21:22-34, Abraham enters a covenant with Abimelech, the king of Gerar, to settle a dispute over a well, a conflict that had simmered beneath the surface of their relationship. The well was a matter of survival in the arid region of Gerar, where water was scarce and precious. Abraham, a newcomer to the land after leaving Haran and traveling through Canaan, had settled temporarily in Gerar with his growing household and vast flocks. To sustain them, he dug wells, tapping into the life-giving water beneath the desert. However, tensions arose when Abimelech's servants seized one of these wells, claiming it as their own. This act of aggression threatened Abraham's ability to thrive in the land and challenged his right to dwell there peacefully alongside the local inhabitants.

Recognizing Abraham's prosperity and the favor he seemed to enjoy from God, Abimelech approached him to propose a covenant. He sought mutual respect and peace, acknowledging that Abraham was no ordinary sojourner. To formalize their agreement, Abraham and Abimelech swore an oath, and Abraham offered seven ewe lambs to Abimelech as a witness to their pact, an act that confirmed Abraham's rightful claim to the well while establishing a lasting alliance. After swearing mutual peace, the text notes,

"Abraham planted a tamarisk tree in Beersheba, and there called on
the name of the Lord, the Everlasting God." (Genesis 21:33)

Most readers might overlook the significance of this detail, but it's a profound example of a covenant marker. The tamarisk, a hardy tree well-suited to arid lands, stood as a living witness to their agreement, its roots symbolically claiming the well as a testament to peace for years to come.

For Abraham's descendants, this tree was more than a physical landmark, it was a legacy of their forefather's faithfulness and diplomacy. As they passed by Beersheba in future generations, they would see the tamarisk and recall the day Abraham secured their right to the land through covenant, a tangible reminder of God's provision and the importance of maintaining peaceful relations with their neighbors. The planting of the tree also carried a deeper significance: just as it took root in the harsh desert soil, God's promises to Abraham, to make him a great nation and a blessing to others (Genesis 12:2-3), were steadily taking root through moments like these. The tamarisk stood as a symbol of endurance and hope, reflecting both the covenant's strength and God's unwavering faithfulness to Abraham and his lineage.

JOSHUA'S COVENANT RENEWAL

Another example emerges in Joshua 24, where Joshua renews Israel's covenant with God at Shechem to reaffirm the nation's commitment to God after their conquest of Canaan, a critical moment when their faith faced new challenges. This renewal was a deliberate response to the spiritual and societal shifts Israel experienced as they transitioned from a wandering people to a settled nation. After years of battles and victories, the Israelites were now in possession of the Promised Land, a land rich with opportunity but also rife with the dangers of idolatry and complacency. Joshua, now aged and nearing the end of his leadership, sought to anchor their faith before he departed. He recounted God's faithfulness, from Abraham's call to their recent victories, and challenged them:

"Choose for yourselves this day whom you will serve... But as for me and my house, we will serve the Lord." (Joshua 24:15)

After the people pledged:

"The Lord our God we will serve, and His voice we will obey!" (Joshua 24:24)

Joshua takes action:

"So Joshua made a covenant with the people that day, and made for them a statute and an ordinance in Shechem...he took a large stone, and set it up there under the oak that was by the sanctuary of the Lord. And Joshua said to all the people, 'Behold, this stone shall be a witness to us, for it has heard all the words of the Lord which He spoke to us. It shall therefore be a witness to you, lest you deny your God.'" (Joshua 24:25-27)

This stone, rooted in sacred soil, echoed the custom of planting trees or raising memorials to ensure that the covenant's memory endured. Just as a tree's growth mirrors a living promise, the oak's enduring presence amplified the stone's testimony, binding Israel's commitment to the land and to future generations.

These acts transcended the immediate participants, embedding the covenant in the landscape itself. When future generations, struck by the sight of stones stacked deliberately in a place where nature left no such mark, would ask, "Why are these stones here?" an elder would seize the moment to retell the story of Shechem. They would speak of Joshua's bold charge to choose whom they would serve, the people's resounding pledge to follow the Lord alone, and how these very stones stood as silent witnesses to that sacred vow (Joshua 24:27). Much like Deuteronomy 6:20-21 (NIV) envisions:

> *"In the future, when your son asks you, 'What is the meaning of the stipulations, decrees and laws the Lord our God has commanded you?' tell him: 'We were slaves of Pharaoh in Egypt, but the Lord brought us out.'"*

More than a marker of history, the stones would stir a living call, urging each new generation to embrace their identity as God's people and renew the covenant etched into their heritage.

For God's people, planting a tree or raising a heap of stones carried profound spiritual weight. These acts symbolized the covenant's longevity, a promise not just for today but for tomorrow. They mirrored God's own nature. Psalm 1:3 likens the righteous to,

> *"a tree planted by the rivers of water, that brings forth its fruit in its season, whose leaf also shall not wither,"*

while 1 Peter 2:5 calls believers,

> *"living stones,"*

being built into a spiritual house. The tree embodied life, growth, and permanence, while the stones spoke of strength and steadfastness, qualities God wove into His covenants. When Abraham planted the tamarisk, he marked his covenant with Abimelech, just as Jacob and Laban piled stones to seal their truce, calling it "Galeed", a witness to their peace.

THE CROSS: OUR GENERATIONAL MEMORIAL

Today, we don't plant trees or heap stones to seal our faith, but the principle persists. The cross, often called a *"tree"* in Scripture (Acts 5:30),

> *"The God of our fathers raised up Jesus whom you murdered by hanging on a tree,"*

stands as our covenant memorial, planted on Golgotha 2,000 years ago. This is reiterated in Galatians 3:13:

> *"Christ has redeemed us from the curse of the law, having become a curse for us, for it is written: 'Cursed is everyone who hangs on a tree.'"*

Yet, Jesus is also the,

> *"living stone,"* (1 Peter 2:4)

the cornerstone of our faith (Ephesians 2:20). That tree of death became life for us, and that stone, rejected by men, became the foundation of a new covenant that spans generations. Every church steeple echoes the tree, every cornerstone of our sanctuaries recalls the stones, reminding us of the blood that sealed our bond with God. And just as Israel's children were to ask about the Law, we're called to teach our children the story of the cross and the cornerstone, why they stand, what they mean, and how they invite us into God's family.

The planting of a tree or the raising of stones sealed the covenant with a legacy. They were quiet, enduring witnesses, ensuring the agreement wasn't forgotten when voices faded. As we'll see next, these memorials found their companion in a ritual of fellowship that bound hearts as surely as roots gripped the earth or stones held their place.

RITUAL 10 – SHARING A MEAL

The tenth and final custom of covenant-making was the sharing of a meal, typically bread and wine, a ritual that sealed the bond with the warmth of fellowship. In the ancient world, to eat with someone was to declare peace, to weave your lives together in a shared act of trust. Bread, the staff of life, and wine, the joy of the vine, symbolized the sustenance and delight that flowed from the covenant, uniting the partners as one.

Scripture abounds with covenant meals, each a testament to the power of shared sustenance in sealing sacred bonds, revealing the unified yet distinct roles of the Father, Son, and Holy Spirit in God's redemptive plan. In Genesis 26:26-31, Isaac and Abimelech, the king of Gerar, renew the peace their fathers—Abraham and an earlier Abimelech—had established. To avoid confusion, it's important to clarify that Abraham and Isaac dealt with two different Abimelechs. The Abimelech in Isaac's time was not the same individual Abraham encountered decades earlier in Genesis 21, but likely a successor or another ruler bearing the same title. Scholars suggest "Abimelech" may have been a dynastic name for the Philistine kings of Gerar, much like "Pharaoh" in Egypt, explaining why both father and son interacted with a king by that name.

ISAAC AND ABIMELECH

Isaac was a sojourner in Gerar, a fertile yet foreign land, where his prosperity, blessed by God with flourishing crops and expanding flocks, ignited envy among the Philistines. This tension erupted when the Philistines stopped up the wells Abraham had dug, claiming the scarce water resources for themselves, a direct threat to Isaac's livelihood in that arid region. Rather than retaliate, Isaac relocated and dug new wells, only to face further disputes as the Philistines contested these too. Amid this friction, the current Abimelech, who was the ruling authority over the Philistines, approached Isaac with a proposal to reaffirm the alliance their predecessors had forged.

They swore not to harm each other, echoing the covenant Abraham had made with the earlier Abimelech. Abraham had already planted a tamarisk tree in Beer-sheba to signify the covenant he established with the original Abimelech, creating a living symbol of their peace rooted in the land (Genesis 21:33). Years later, when Isaac encountered a new Abimelech, the covenant his father had marked with the tree still stood as the foundation of their relationship. This next generation, Isaac and the new Abimelech, needed only to reaffirm this existing agreement rather than forge a new one. However, because Isaac was dealing with a different Abimelech, a mere oath might have felt insufficient to ensure lasting peace across the shifting dynamics of time. Words alone could seem fleeting, lacking the weight to bridge the generations. To solidify their commitment,

> *"Isaac then made a feast for them, and they ate and drank. Early the next morning the men swore an oath to each other. Then Isaac sent them on their way, and they went away peacefully."* (Genesis 26:30-31, NIV)

This feast, a culturally significant ritual, reaffirmed the covenant Abraham's tree had first signified, breathing fresh life into their alliance and making it tangible for their era through the shared act of fellowship.

COVENANTAL MEAL AT SINAI

Similarly, in Exodus 24:9-11 (NIV), after God confirms the Sinai covenant with blood,

> *"Moses and Aaron, Nadab and Abihu, and the seventy elders of Israel went up and saw the God of Israel... But God did not raise his hand against these leaders of the Israelites; they saw God, and they ate and drank."*

This extraordinary moment, dining in God's presence, marked the covenant's sealing, a foretaste of the fellowship Israel could enjoy as His people. Theologically, this meal reflects communion with the Father, the sovereign covenant-maker who initiates His relationship with Israel. As Deuteronomy 32:6 and Isaiah 64:8 portray God as the Father who forms and calls His people, this Sinai feast signifies His gracious invitation to dwell with Him, establishing the foundation of covenantal fellowship. The Father's presence, revealed in this theophany, underscores His role as the source of the covenant, though the Son and Spirit are ever-present in the Trinity's unified work, ensuring the sacredness of this encounter.

To fully appreciate this event, we must consider the broader narrative of Exodus 24, where the Sinai covenant unfolds as a carefully structured process. It begins with God's dramatic revelation of the Ten Commandments in Exodus 20, a moment that establishes His authority and holiness. The people, awestruck, respond through Moses with a collective pledge:

> *"All the words which the Lord has said we will do."* (Exodus 24:3)

Moses then records these terms in the *Book of the Covenant,* reads it aloud to the assembly, and receives their renewed commitment:

> *"All that the Lord has said we will do, and be obedient."* (Exodus 24:7)

To ratify this solemn agreement, Moses conducts a blood ritual, sacrificing young bulls and sprinkling half the blood on the altar (symbolizing God's part) and half on the people (symbolizing their part), declaring,

> *"This is the blood of the covenant which the Lord has made with you."* (Exodus 24:8)

This act underscores the life-and-death stakes of the covenant, a bond sealed in blood.

Yet, the covenant process reaches its climax not with blood alone but with the shared meal that follows. At Sinai, God takes this custom to a divine level, inviting Moses, Aaron, Nadab, Abihu, and the seventy elders to ascend the mountain and dine in His presence. The text marvels that they,

"saw the God of Israel," (Exodus 24:10)

a rare and dangerous privilege, given God's warning that no one can see Him and live (Exodus 33:20)—and yet,

"God did not raise his hand against these leaders." (Exodus 24:11)

This grace-filled encounter, centered on the Father's initiative, culminates in their eating and drinking before Him, an act that seals the covenant and embodies the intimate relationship He seeks with His people. The significance of this meal extends beyond its historical moment, pointing to the work of the Son in the New Covenant.

THE DISCIPLES COVENANTAL MEAL WITH JESUS

On the night before His crucifixion, Jesus gathers His disciples for the Passover, a meal already rich with covenant echoes of deliverance from Egypt. He takes bread, gives thanks, breaks it, and says,

"This is My body which is given for you; do this in remembrance of Me." (Luke 22:19)

Then He takes the cup, saying,

"This cup is the new covenant in My blood, which is shed for you."
(Luke 22:20)

Here, Jesus, the mediator of the New Covenant (Hebrews 12:24), establishes a meal centered on His sacrificial death and resurrection. The bread, broken as His body would be, and the wine, poured out as His blood, seal the New Covenant, not with animal sacrifice, but with the Lamb of God Himself. This meal, defined by the Son's redemptive act, surpasses the Sinai feast, as it reconciles humanity to God through Christ's atoning work. While the Father and Spirit are united with the Son in this moment, it is Jesus' initiative and presence that anchor this covenant meal, inviting believers into communion with Him.

Paul later writes,

"For as often as you eat this bread and drink this cup, you proclaim the Lord's death till He comes," (1 Corinthians 11:26)

tying this meal to the cross and the promise of Christ's return. This promise points ultimately to the wedding feast of the Lamb, described in Revelation 19:9, where the angel declares,

"Blessed are those who are called to the marriage supper of the Lamb!"

This heavenly banquet is the culmination of the covenant meals throughout Scripture, where the covenant fellowship initiated at Sinai and renewed at the Last Supper will be eternally celebrated. While centered on Christ the Bridegroom, this feast reflects the work of the Holy Spirit, who prepares and sanctifies the Church as His Bride (Ephesians 5:25-27) and seals believers for the day of redemption (Ephesians 1:13-14). The Spirit, who guides us into all truth and glorifies Christ (John 16:13-14), enables our participation in this eternal communion, bringing the covenant to its glorious consummation. The Father's plan and the

Son's sacrifice converge in this feast, but it is the Spirit's transformative presence that unites the Church, ready to dine with the Bridegroom in glory. Thus, the Sinai meal (with the Father), the Last Supper (with the Son), and the Wedding Feast (with the Holy Spirit) form a continuum, each revealing God's progressive invitation to dwell with His people in ever-deepening intimacy, reflecting the unified yet distinct roles of the Trinity across salvation history.

At Sinai, the elders of Israel experienced a glimpse of divine fellowship, dining in the Father's presence as the covenant was sealed. At the Last Supper, Jesus invited His followers into a deeper communion through His sacrifice, establishing the New Covenant through the Son. Yet both meals anticipated the greater reality of the Wedding Feast, where believers will join Christ in perfect, eternal fellowship, empowered by the Holy Spirit's sanctifying work.

In the New Covenant, communion is our covenant meal, a sacred act that seals our union with Christ and one another, embodying the Trinitarian love that binds us to God. When we partake, we're not just remembering history; we're renewing our place in the covenant established by the Son, initiated by the Father, and sustained by the Spirit. The bread unites us as Christ's body (1 Corinthians 10:17), the wine cleanses us by His blood (Hebrews 9:14), and together they proclaim our shared life in Him—a life rooted in the Father's eternal plan and empowered by the Spirit's indwelling presence. Communion is a moment of intimacy, a foretaste of the Wedding Feast where we'll dine with the Bridegroom in glory (Revelation 19:9), made possible by the Spirit's work in our hearts. Yet, it's also a call to examine ourselves (1 Corinthians 11:28), ensuring we approach this table in faith and unity, honoring the covenant sealed by the Triune God's redemptive love.

GENESIS 31: THE STORY OF JACOB AND LABAN

As we've explored the rituals that defined ancient covenants—reading the terms, planting a tree or raising a memorial, and sharing a meal—we find a powerful illustration in the story of Jacob and Laban from Genesis 31. Their covenant, born out of tension and sealed in the hills of Gilead, brings together all three elements, offering a vivid example of how these practices forged a lasting bond and restored peace between two estranged men.

The relationship between Jacob and Laban began decades earlier, when Jacob fled to Haran to escape his brother Esau's wrath after deceiving him out of his birthright and blessing (Genesis 27:41-45). Arriving at his uncle Laban's home, Jacob sought refuge and soon fell in love with Laban's younger daughter, Rachel. He agreed to work seven years for her hand in marriage, but Laban tricked him, giving him Leah instead on the wedding night:

> *"When morning came, there was Leah! So Jacob said to Laban, 'What is this you have done to me? I served you for Rachel, didn't I? Why have you deceived me?'"* (Genesis 29:25, NIV)

Laban's excuse was a custom of the time, and he offered Rachel too, for another seven years of labor (Genesis 29:27-28). This betrayal set the tone for their relationship.

Over 20 years, Jacob worked tirelessly, tending Laban's flocks, despite Laban's repeated deceit. He changed Jacob's wages ten times:

> *"Yet your father has deceived me and changed my wages ten times,"* (v.7)

yet God blessed Jacob abundantly. His flocks grew through a shrewd breeding strategy (Genesis 30:37-43), and his wealth increased, as did his family, with eleven sons and a daughter born to Leah, Rachel, and their servants (Genesis 30:1-24). This prosperity, however, fueled Laban's jealousy:

> *"Now Jacob heard the words of Laban's sons, saying, 'Jacob has taken away all that was our father's, and from what was our father's he has*

acquired all this wealth.' And Jacob saw the countenance of Laban,
and indeed it was not favorable toward him as before." (vv.1-2)

Fearing for his safety and prompted by God's command,

"Then the Lord said to Jacob, 'Return to the land of your fathers and
to your family, and I will be with you.'" (v.3)

Jacob fled with his wives, children, and livestock. Laban, enraged, pursued him,
accusing Jacob of stealing his household gods:

"Why did you flee away secretly, and steal away from me, and not
tell me; for I might have sent you away with joy and songs…? why did
you steal my gods?" (vv.27, 30)

This confrontation, seven days later in the hills of Gilead, teetered on the edge
of violence. But God intervened, warning Laban in a dream:

"Be careful that you speak to Jacob neither good nor bad." (v.24)

This divine protection shifted the encounter toward peace.

Rather than fight, Jacob and Laban chose to make a covenant, enacting three
rituals that transformed their conflict into commitment. The covenant began
with a tangible sign. Laban proposed,

"Come, let us make a covenant, you and I, and let it be a witness
between you and me." (v.44)

Jacob responded decisively:

"So Jacob took a stone and set it up as a pillar. Then Jacob said to his brethren, 'Gather stones.' And they took stones and made a heap, and they ate there on the heap." (vv.45-46)

This heap of stones, alongside the solitary pillar, served as a monument and a witness to their agreement etched into the landscape. Named "Galeed" (meaning "witness pile") and "Mizpah" (meaning "watchtower"), it stood as a lasting reminder of their promise, a physical testament for generations to see.

With the memorial established, Jacob and Laban turned to the terms of their pact. Laban declared,

"This heap is a witness between you and me this day," (v.48)

and set his conditions:

"If you afflict my daughters, or if you take other wives besides my daughters, although no man is with us—see, God is witness between you and me." (v.50)

Jacob then added his own commitment:

"This heap is a witness, and this pillar is a witness, that I will not pass beyond this heap to you, and you will not pass beyond this heap and this pillar to me, for harm." (v.52)

They sealed their words by invoking divine oversight:

"The God of Abraham, the God of Nahor, and the God of their father judge between us." (v.53)

These terms, spoken clearly and publicly, bound them to mutual respect and accountability.

Finally, they cemented their covenant with a meal,

"And they ate there on the heap." (v.46)

Jacob went further and,

"offered a sacrifice on the mountain, and called his brethren to eat bread. And they ate bread and stayed all night on the mountain." (v.54)

In that shared act of breaking bread, following a sacrifice to God, what had been a relationship of suspicion became one of fellowship. The meal transformed their words and stones into a living bond, a moment of peace amidst the hills.

Through these acts—raising a stone witness, speaking words of commitment, and sharing a meal—Jacob and Laban turned enmity into alliance. Their story reveals God's pattern for reconciliation, woven into creation itself: stones that endure, words that clarify, and bread that unites. In Christ, we see this pattern fulfilled: the cross as our eternal memorial, His law written on our hearts, and His table as our sacred fellowship. As we live in this New Covenant, may we embrace these rituals as a call to trust, remember, and dwell in God's reconciling love.

THREE WAYS GOD CONNECTS WITH YOU IN COVENANT

When Jesus died on the cross and rose from the dead, the New Covenant was created between God and every person who ever existed from that point forward. Only when we accept Jesus Christ as our savior, do we step into the New Covenant. However, the secret of the Lord, or all the benefits of the New Covenant, is not revealed until we live a life of fearing God.□

You'll know when the secret of the Lord has been revealed to you when you understand when God is speaking directly to you such as a friend would. When you start seeing miracles being worked in your life, you'll know God has remembered the promises of His New Covenant. Finally, God's grace is available to all and He shows us lovingkindness when we stumble.□

TERM 1 – FRIEND
TERM 2 – REMEMBER
TERM 3 – LOVINGKINDNESS

CHAPTER 9

FRIENDS OF GOD

With the foundation of the ten rituals of covenant-making now firmly in place, we turn our attention to a deeper layer of God's covenantal language in Scripture. There are three essential terms God employs to express the heart of His covenants: "friend," "remember," and "lovingkindness."

When the secret of the Lord is revealed to you, you'll see how you too are a friend of God, invited into His intimate covenantal circle through faith and obedience. You'll recognize how He remembers His covenant with you, faithfully upholding His promises across generations, and even in your failings. His lovingkindness, His steadfast, unfailing mercy, is there to pick you back up, restoring you with grace that never wavers. These words are divine keys that unlock the relational depth and enduring nature of God's promises.

In the modern day, "friend" often denotes superficial connections like social media acquaintances or someone you know but don't spend much time with. In the Bible, God uses the word "friend" as a covenantal bond rich with loyalty and intimacy which we often overlook. So in the Bible, when you see "friend", you're supposed to think covenant. It's not about surface-level companionship; it's about a profound, enduring bond that reflects God's own faithfulness. Consider Proverbs 17:17:

"A friend loves at all times, And a brother is born for adversity."

This isn't a friend who's only around when it's convenient. A biblical friend loves you *"at all times,"* through joy, struggle, and even disagreement. Imagine correcting a friend, saying, "You should not do that," and instead of taking offense, they listen and remain steadfast. That's the kind of friendship Scripture celebrates, a love that holds firm, no matter the circumstances.

This covenantal friendship is also a two-way street. Proverbs 18:24 puts it plainly:

"A man who has friends must himself be friendly."

If you want friends who embody this deep commitment, you must first be that kind of friend yourself. It's an active, intentional choice to love and support others, mirroring the loyalty God shows His people.

In this chapter, we'll uncover the covenantal essence of friendship in the Bible. We'll see how "friend" goes beyond our cultural understanding, revealing a sacred relationship that echoes God's covenant with humanity. Get ready to explore what it truly means to be a friend in God's design, a bond that's unshakable, reciprocal, and rooted in divine love.

GOD'S FRIEND ABRAHAM

In the Bible, Abraham stands out as a remarkable figure, not just as a patriarch or a man of faith, but as someone God Himself calls *"My friend."* In Isaiah 41:8, God declares,

"But you, Israel, are My servant, Jacob whom I have chosen, The descendants of Abraham My friend."

God isn't throwing around the word *"friend"* lightly; it's a profound statement of intimacy. Similarly, James 2:23 affirms this bond:

> *"And the Scripture was fulfilled which says, 'Abraham believed God, and it was accounted to him for righteousness.' And he was called the friend of God."*

What made Abraham God's friend? It wasn't just his belief, though that was central, it was his active, lived-out faith, his obedience through unimaginable trials, and the mutual trust that defined his relationship with the Almighty.

Abraham's friendship with God was forged in the fires of a divine covenant, detailed in Genesis 15. Abraham's trust in God was the heartbeat of their friendship, a trust that shone through every step of his journey. When God called him to leave Ur, his homeland, for an unknown destination (Genesis 12:1-4), Abraham didn't hesitate, he went, leaving behind familiarity for faith. Years later, God promised him a son, Isaac, despite his and Sarah's advanced age. Decades passed, yet Abraham held fast, trusting God's word when all logic screamed otherwise. Then came the ultimate test: God asked him to sacrifice Isaac, the long-awaited child of promise (Genesis 22). Without bargaining or delay, Abraham rose early, took his son to Mount Moriah, and prepared to obey, believing God could even raise the dead (Hebrews 11:17-19). Abraham didn't simply submit to this; he was showing the loyalty of a friend who knows God's character. Abraham loved God unwaveringly, standing firm when life darkened, proving his friendship through action.

This friendship wasn't one-sided, God reciprocated with remarkable openness. In Genesis 18, we see a stunning moment of divine vulnerability. As God considers destroying Sodom for its wickedness, He pauses and reflects,

"Shall I hide from Abraham what I am doing, since Abraham shall surely become a great and mighty nation, and all the nations of the earth shall be blessed in him?" (Genesis 18:17-18)

Deciding against secrecy, God shares His plans, inviting Abraham into a conversation about justice and mercy. Abraham responds boldly yet humbly, interceding for the righteous in Sodom:

"Would You also destroy the righteous with the wicked? ... Shall not the Judge of all the earth do right?" (Genesis 18:23-25)

This exchange reveals a profound privilege, God didn't treat Abraham as a servant, but as a confidant, a partner privy to His heart. It's the kind of openness that defines true friendship, where thoughts and intentions are shared freely.

Abraham's friendship with God was a covenantal bond built on mutual commitment. His faith wasn't passive; it was a dynamic trust that moved him to act, whether leaving home, waiting for Isaac, or climbing Moriah. God, in turn, honored that trust with intimacy, revealing His plans and listening to Abraham's pleas. This relationship reflects the essence of biblical friendship: loyalty that endures adversity, faith that trusts beyond reason, and a closeness that invites dialogue with the divine. When God calls Abraham *"My friend,"* it's a testament to a life lived in faithful partnership, a model for us all.

JEHOSHAPHAT'S PLEA

Centuries later, King Jehoshaphat of Judah echoes a profound understanding of covenantal friendship, demonstrating its power in one of the nation's darkest hours. In 2 Chronicles 20, Judah confronts a dire military threat from a formidable coalition of enemy nations. The armies of the Moabites, Ammonites, and Edomites—peoples with a history of enmity toward Israel—unite and march against Judah, their combined forces overwhelming in number and strength.

This was an existential crisis, with Judah's survival hanging in the balance. Outnumbered and outmatched, the small kingdom faced the very real prospect of annihilation.

In this moment of desperation, King Jehoshaphat does not turn to conventional solutions. He does not scramble to bolster his military defenses, seek alliances with neighboring powers, or devise a clever strategy to outmaneuver the enemy. Instead, he turns to God. Recognizing Judah's utter powerlessness, Jehoshaphat proclaims a fast throughout the land and gathers the people, men, women, and children, to seek the Lord's help. Standing in the temple before this assembly, he cries out to God with raw honesty:

> *"We have no power against this great multitude that is coming against us; nor do we know what to do, but our eyes are upon You."* (2 Chronicles 20:12)

His words paint a vivid picture of vulnerability, like a baby bird chirping helplessly in its nest, unable to fend for itself against a looming predator.

It is within this prayer that Jehoshaphat makes a remarkable appeal, grounding his plea in the covenant God made with Abraham centuries earlier. He prays,

> *"Are You not our God, who drove out the inhabitants of this land before Your people Israel, and gave it to the descendants of Abraham Your friend forever?"* (2 Chronicles 20:7)

This is a deliberate invocation of a sacred relationship. By calling Abraham *"Your friend,"* Jehoshaphat highlights the personal, intimate bond that defines God's covenant with Abraham. He's essentially saying, "Lord, You're our God, and I recall that You have a covenant with our father Abraham. Not a temporary agreement that lasted for four or five generations, but a promise that endures forever. You bound Yourself to him as his friend, and we are his descendants."

This plea is steeped in the language of covenantal friendship. Jehoshaphat's words carry the urgency of a child appealing to a parent's promise: "This army is too big for us. We cannot defend ourselves against this enemy. But You are our God. We are Your people, and we have a covenant with You. Remember Abraham, Your friend forever." He acknowledges Judah's helplessness while simultaneously clinging to the eternal commitment God made to Abraham, a commitment that extends to all his heirs, including the people of Judah standing before Him then.

The power of this appeal lies in its foundation: the enduring nature of covenantal friendship. God's relationship with Abraham was a solemn pact, sealed with promises of land, protection, and blessing for all generations (Genesis 17:7-8). By invoking this, Jehoshaphat shifts the focus from Judah's weakness to God's faithfulness. He's not bargaining or begging from a place of uncertainty; he's standing on the solid ground of a divine promise, trusting that the God who called Abraham His friend will honor that bond.

And God does. In a stunning response, He speaks through the prophet Jahaziel, declaring,

> "Do not be afraid nor dismayed because of this great multitude, for the battle is not yours, but God's." (2 Chronicles 20:15)

The next day, as Judah's army marches out, not to fight, but to worship, they lift their voices in praise to God. In a miraculous turn of events, the Lord sets an ambush against the enemy coalition. The Moabites, Ammonites, and Edomites turn on one another, destroying themselves in confusion while Judah watches in awe. The victory is complete and decisive, achieved without Judah lifting a sword. The vast army that threatened their existence is reduced to a field of corpses, a testament to God's power and His fidelity to His covenant.

This extraordinary deliverance reveals the depth of covenantal friendship. Jehoshaphat's prayer was not a desperate shot in the dark, it was a confident appeal to a relationship initiated and upheld by God Himself. The routing of the enemy without Judah's military intervention underscores that their salvation came not from human effort but from divine intervention, a direct fulfillment of the promise made to Abraham, God's friend. For Jehoshaphat and the people of Judah, this victory was a living reminder that their hope rested not in their own strength, but in the unbreakable bond of covenant that stretched back to their forefather Abraham.

MOSES: A FACE-TO-FACE FRIEND TO GOD

Moses, too, embodies the essence of biblical friendship as a covenantal bond. Exodus 33:11 declares,

"So the Lord spoke to Moses face to face, as a man speaks to his friend."

This striking description highlights an extraordinary intimacy between God and Moses, where God engages Moses with a directness and familiarity that mirrors the closeness of human friendship. The phrase *"face to face"* signifies an unfiltered, honest exchange, one where trust and mutual understanding flow freely. This covenantal bond, rooted in God's faithfulness and Moses' bold faith, empowered him to accomplish remarkable feats, from leading Israel out of Egypt to interceding for their survival in moments of divine judgment.

This intimacy is most vividly displayed in the aftermath of Israel's rebellion with the golden calf in Exodus 32. When the people, freshly delivered from Egypt, turn to idolatry, God's anger burns fiercely:

"Now therefore, let Me alone, that My wrath may burn hot against them and I may consume them. And I will make of you a great nation." (Exodus 32:10)

The threat is dire, God is prepared to wipe out Israel and start anew with Moses. Yet, Moses does not shrink from this moment; instead, he steps into the breach as an intercessor, embodying the covenantal friendship that binds him to God. He pleads,

> *"Remember Abraham, Isaac, and Israel, Your servants, to whom You swore by Your own self, and said to them, 'I will multiply your descendants as the stars of heaven; and all this land that I have spoken of I give to your descendants, and they shall inherit it forever.'"* (Exodus 32:13)

This bold appeal is not a negotiation but a confident invocation of God's covenant with Abraham, rooted in Moses' deep understanding of God's character. His words move God to relent:

> *"So the Lord relented from the harm which He said He would do to His people."* (Exodus 32:14)

Through this act of intercession, Moses accomplishes something remarkable: he secures mercy for a rebellious nation, standing as a mediator between God's justice and Israel's sin. Speaking *"face to face"* with God equips Moses with the authority and insight to navigate this crisis, reflecting a friendship where trust and honesty flow freely. Moses' closeness to God becomes a channel for divine grace, illustrating how such a relationship enables one to fulfill God's redemptive purposes even amidst human failure.

Moses' friendship with God was not limited to this singular moment of intercession. His role as Israel's leader required ongoing communion with the divine, and God's willingness to engage him directly underscores the depth of their bond. In Numbers 12:6-8 (ESV), God defends Moses against Aaron and Miriam's criticism, declaring,

> *"With him I speak mouth to mouth, clearly, and not in riddles, and he beholds the form of the Lord."*

This divine affirmation sets Moses apart from other prophets, emphasizing the clarity and intimacy of their communication. This closeness enabled Moses to accomplish extraordinary tasks: he received the Law on Mount Sinai (Exodus 20), guided Israel through the wilderness despite their complaints (Exodus 16-17), and stood as God's spokesperson, delivering His words with authority. His face-to-face encounters with God, particularly in the tent of meeting (Exodus 33:7-11), were not just moments of personal privilege but opportunities to align Israel with God's will, shaping them into a covenant people.

The significance of Moses' friendship with God extends beyond his own actions, it reflects the covenantal nature of their relationship. Like Abraham, Moses was privy to God's heart, as seen when God invited him to intercede and revealed His glory in response to Moses' request:

"Please, show me your glory." (Exodus 33:18, ESV)

God's response,

"I will make all my goodness pass before you and will proclaim before you my name 'The Lord,'" (Exodus 33:19, ESV)

reveals a level of openness reserved for a friend. This moment, where God partially unveils His glory while shielding Moses in the cleft of the rock, underscores the trust and intimacy that defined their bond. Moses' ability to intercede, lead, and commune with God was not rooted in his own merit but in the covenantal relationship God initiated.

Moses' friendship with God also had a transformative impact on Israel. His intercession didn't just save them from destruction; it preserved their identity as God's chosen people, bound by the covenant established with Abraham and renewed through the Law. His leadership—guiding them out of Egypt, through the Red Sea, and toward the Promised Land—was empowered by this friendship, which gave him the courage to face Pharaoh, the faith to trust God's provision, and the authority to mediate God's presence. Even when Israel grumbled or rebelled, Moses' loyalty to both God and His people reflected the steadfast love of a friend who,

"loves at all times." (Proverbs 17:17)

His life shows that covenantal friendship with God is not a static privilege but a dynamic relationship that equips one to fulfill divine purposes, even amidst human failure.

Moses' remarkable friendship with God, marked by face-to-face communion and bold intercession, set a high standard for what it means to be a covenantal friend. His life of sacrifice and leadership, sustained by God's intimate presence, paved the way for Israel's covenantal identity. Yet, this sacred bond of friendship finds its ultimate fulfillment in Jesus, who takes the concept even further. In the New Testament, Jesus redefines the relationship between God and His people, moving from the intimacy of a chosen mediator like Moses to a broader invitation for all disciples to become friends of God. This shift, rooted in the new covenant, opens a new chapter in the story of divine friendship, where trust and partnership reach their pinnacle through Christ's revelation and sacrifice.

FROM SERVANTS TO FRIENDS

In the Gospel of John, during his farewell discourse, Jesus redefines his relationship with his disciples in a profound way. He declares in John 15:15,

"No longer do I call you servants, for a servant does not know what his master is doing; but I have called you friends, for all things that I heard from My Father I have made known to you."

This statement marks a significant shift: Jesus elevates his disciples from servants, who follow orders without understanding the bigger picture, to friends, who are entrusted with the intimate knowledge of God's plan. This friendship is a covenantal relationship, reflecting the deep trust God extended to figures like Abraham and Moses in the Old Testament. Yet, this does not negate the broader reality that all believers remain servants of Christ, bought by his blood (1 Corinthians 6:20). Jesus' words introduce a new layer of connection, one of partnership and purpose.

Jesus didn't just call his disciples friends; he equipped them with remarkable authority to act in his name. This empowerment is evident throughout the Gospels. In Matthew 10:1, Jesus summoned his twelve disciples and grants them specific powers:

> *"And when He had called His twelve disciples to Him, He gave them power over unclean spirits, to cast them out, and to heal all kinds of sickness and all kinds of disease."*

This moment transformed the disciples from passive followers into active participants in Jesus' ministry, capable of performing miracles that mirror his own works. They are no longer just learners; they are doers, extending God's healing and deliverance to those in need.

The scope of this authority expands further in John 14:12, where Jesus made a striking promise:

> *"Most assuredly, I say to you, he who believes in Me, the works that I do he will do also; and greater works than these he will do, because I go to My Father."*

This statement is astonishing, Jesus suggested that the disciples' ministry will exceed his own earthly deeds. How is this possible? The key lies in his departure to the Father, which paves the way for the coming of the Holy Spirit at Pentecost. Empowered by the Spirit, the disciples' reach and impact will grow beyond what Jesus accomplished in his physical ministry, as they spread the gospel to all nations.

The death and resurrection of Jesus are the cornerstone of this friendship and the authority it carries. Through His sacrificial death on the cross, Jesus redeemed humanity, securing forgiveness and establishing a new covenant. This act not only saves but also commissions His disciples as friends and co-laborers in God's redemptive work. The resurrection amplifies this further, it is the ultimate proof of Jesus' authority over sin and death, and it validates the mission He entrusted to His disciples. When Jesus rises, He appears to them and declares,

> *"And Jesus came and spoke to them, saying, 'All authority has been given to Me in heaven and on earth. Go therefore and make disciples of all the nations, baptizing them in the name of the Father and of the Son and of the Holy Spirit, teaching them to observe all things that I have commanded you.'"* (Matthew 28:18-20)

Known as the Great Commission, this charge is a direct outflow of His resurrection power, linking their authority to His triumph.

The cross and empty tomb transform the disciples' understanding of their role. Before the crucifixion, they struggled to grasp Jesus' mission; after the resurrection, they saw clearly that their friendship with Him was a call to action. His death purchased their redemption, and His resurrection empowered them to carry His message forward, equipped by the Holy Spirit to heal, teach, and reconcile a broken world to God.

Jesus' declaration of friendship, the authority He granted, and His death and resurrection are intricately connected. Calling the disciples *"friends"* is not just a sentimental gesture, it's an invitation into God's mission. The authority to heal diseases, cast out demons, and perform *"greater works"* flows from Jesus' identity as the Son of God, proven through His resurrection. His death breaks the power of sin, making reconciliation possible, while His resurrection ensures that His disciples can continue His work with divine backing. This friendship is both a privilege and a responsibility, as the disciples, and all believers, are called to embody Christ's love and power in the world. To be a friend of Jesus is to share in His authority and mission. Just as the disciples were empowered to act in His name, so too are we, through the same Spirit, invited to participate in God's redemptive plan. It's a relationship that redefines our purpose and equips us to live boldly for Him.

TRUST AND TRANSFORMATION FROM FRIENDSHIP

In the pages of Scripture, the term *"friend"* emerges not as a casual label, but as a profound covenantal bond that reflects the heart of God's relationship with His people. Far beyond our modern notions of friendship, biblical friendship is a sacred partnership, rooted in faith, loyalty, and mutual commitment. Through the lives of Abraham, Jehoshaphat, Moses, and Jesus' disciples, we've seen how this term weaves a consistent thread across the Old and New Testaments, revealing a love that endures adversity and a trust that transforms lives.

Abraham's journey sets the foundation. Called *"My friend"* by God (Isaiah 41:8), his friendship a covenant forged through active faith. Jehoshaphat, centuries later, stood on this same covenantal ground. Facing an overwhelming enemy coalition, he didn't rely on military might but on the promise tied to Abraham, God's friend forever (2 Chronicles 20:7). Moses took this intimacy further, speaking to God,

"face to face, as a man speaks to his friend." (Exodus 33:11)

Finally, Jesus redefined friendship for His disciples, declaring,

"I have called you friends, for all that I have heard from My Father I have made known to you." (John 15:15)

These friendships are both a gift and a call with a love that sacrifices and empowers.

Together, these stories paint a vivid picture: to be a friend of God is to be woven into a covenant, a sacred agreement that demands trust, obedience, and action. Jesus made His disciples friends by elevating them from servants to confidants, entrusting them with the intimate knowledge of the Father's plans and granting them the same authority He wielded—to heal the sick, cast out demons, and proclaim the kingdom of God with power. We too have this same authority as friends of God, empowered by the Holy Spirit to continue His works and do even greater things in His name.

CHAPTER 10

GOD REMEMBERS

In the grand narrative of Scripture, the concept of God "remembering" stands as a profound testament to His unchanging character and unwavering commitment to humanity. Unlike human memory, which is fallible and prone to forgetfulness, God's remembrance is not about recalling something that has slipped His mind, for He is omniscient, eternal, and beyond the limitations of time. Rather, biblical language employs this anthropomorphic term to describe the moment when God actively intervenes in history, fulfilling His promises and demonstrating His mercy. It is a divine act that bridges the eternal with the temporal, turning covenantal pledges into tangible realities.

This chapter explores the theme of remembrance within the framework of God's covenants, drawing from key biblical texts and stories. We will examine how God remembers His covenants—those sacred agreements that define His relationship with creation, from the rainbow-sealed promise to Noah to the mercy-filled New Covenant in Christ. Furthermore, we will consider how Christians, as heirs to these covenants, are called to remember them in their daily lives, worship, and community. While this discussion intersects with the covenantal terms of "friend" and "lovingkindness," our focus remains on remembrance as the mechanism through which God's faithfulness is revealed and reciprocated. Through this lens, remembrance emerges not as a passive recollection but as an active force: for God, it propels salvation history forward; for believers, it anchors faith.

REMEMBRANCE IN THE NOAHIC COVENANT

The Old Testament abounds with instances where God "remembers" His covenants, often at pivotal moments of crisis or transition. These episodes underscore that divine remembrance is synonymous with action, rescue, restoration, and renewal. Let us survey the key narratives and verses that illuminate this theme.

One of the earliest depictions of God's remembrance occurs in the aftermath of the Great Flood, a cataclysmic event that resets creation due to humanity's wickedness (Genesis 6–9). As the waters rage for 150 days, Scripture declares,

> *"Then God remembered Noah, and every living thing, and all the animals that were with him in the ark. And God made a wind to pass over the earth, and the waters subsided."* (Genesis 8:1)

This remembrance initiates the recession of the floodwaters, preserving life and paving the way for a new beginning.

Following the flood, God establishes the Noahic Covenant, promising never again to destroy the earth with a flood. The sign of this covenant, the rainbow, serves as a perpetual reminder:

> *"I will remember my covenant that is between me and you and every living creature of all flesh. And the waters shall never again become a flood to destroy all flesh."* (Genesis 9:15)

Here, the rainbow functions as a visual prompt, not because God needs reminding, but to symbolize His self-imposed commitment. It ties remembrance to God's lovingkindness, which extends to all creation, whether they choose to follow Him or not. This covenant sets a precedent: God's memory safeguards life, blending mercy with justice.

REMEMBRANCE IN THE ABRAHAMIC COVENANT

The Abrahamic Covenant stands as a foundational pillar in the tapestry of God's redemptive plan, a divine promise that reverberates through history and Scripture. In Psalm 105:8-11, we read:

> *"He remembers His covenant forever, The word which He commanded, for a thousand generations, The covenant which He made with Abraham, And His oath to Isaac, And confirmed it to Jacob for a statute, To Israel as an everlasting covenant, Saying, 'To you I will give the land of Canaan As the allotment of your inheritance.'"*

This covenant, first introduced in Genesis 12:1-3 and where God promises to make Abraham a great nation and bless all peoples through him is an eternal pledge, marked God's initiative and faithfulness, setting the stage for His dealings with His people across time. God's promise to Abraham did not end with him, it was intentionally passed down, establishing its enduring nature. The psalm highlights this transmission: it was a *"sworn oath to Isaac"* and *"confirmed to Jacob as a statute."*

In Genesis 26:3-4, God reaffirms the covenant to Isaac, promising the land and numerous descendants. Later, in Genesis 28:13-15, He confirms it to Jacob, tying the promise to the land of Canaan and the lineage of Israel. By calling it an *"everlasting covenant,"* Psalm 105 underscores its permanence, God binds Himself to this commitment forever, ensuring it transcends generations. This continuity establishes Israel's identity as God's chosen people, rooted in a promise that cannot be undone.

The phrase *"He remembers His covenant forever"* shows God's remembrance is active and dynamic. This eternal commitment means that every act of faithfulness flows from His resolve to uphold the covenant. The poetic *"for a thousand generations"* amplifies this, suggesting a faithfulness that outlasts human comprehension. As the psalm unfolds, each event becomes a testament to God's unwavering dedication to the promise first made to Abraham, proving that His covenant is the foundation for all that follows.

Perhaps the most dramatic display of divine remembrance unfolds in the Exodus saga. Enslaved in Egypt, the Israelites groan under oppression:

> *"So God heard their groaning, and God remembered His covenant with Abraham, with Isaac, and with Jacob."* (Exodus 2:24)

In Exodus 6:5, God reaffirms this to Moses:

> *"And I have also heard the groaning of the children of Israel whom the Egyptians keep in bondage, and I have remembered My covenant."*

This divine remembrance was the spark that ignited the Exodus, proving that God's promises are not forgotten but fulfilled in His perfect timing. The events in Egypt, from the plagues to the Exodus, were direct expressions of God's covenant faithfulness. When the psalmist declares,

> *"He remembers His covenant forever,"* (Psalm 105:8)

it encapsulates this active intervention.

Even in warnings of future disobedience, God's remembrance offers hope. He promised that if the people repented, humbling their hearts, He would,

> *"remember My covenant with Jacob, and My covenant with Isaac and My covenant with Abraham."* (Leviticus 26:42)

This assurance extends to His promise:

"For the Lord your God is a merciful God, He will not forsake you nor destroy you, nor forget the covenant of your fathers which He swore to them." (Deuteronomy 4:31)

This promise echoed the earlier assurances in Leviticus 26:42 and 45, reinforcing that God's covenant love would endure. The phrase *"He will not forget the covenant"* emphasizes the negation of forgetfulness, highlighting remembrance as an unbreakable aspect of His covenant, ensuring restoration despite exile or failure.

Psalm 105:42-45 recounts,

"For He remembered His holy promise, And Abraham His servant. He brought out His people with joy, His chosen ones with gladness. He gave them the lands of the Gentiles, And they inherited the labor of the nations, That they might observe His statutes And keep His laws."

This culmination ties remembrance to joy, inheritance, and obedience, illustrating how God's active memory fulfills the Abrahamic Covenant in communal blessing. Through these echoes, the covenant reveals God not as a distant deity but as a faithful friend who remembers and redeems across generations.

ABRAHAM'S FAMILY REMEMBERED

The covenant that God established with Abraham in Genesis 12:1-3, promising land, numerous descendants, and blessing to all nations, forms the bedrock of His redemptive plan, extending far beyond Abraham to touch his family and lineage across generations. This sacred bond manifests in moments where God remembers His promises, acting to preserve, bless, and restore those tied to Abraham's covenantal legacy. From immediate kin to distant heirs, the stories of Lot, Rachel,

Hannah, and Ephraim illustrate how God's commitment to Abraham ripples through time, shaping the lives of individuals and the destiny of Israel. Each instance of divine remembrance underscores the intimate friendship between God and His people, ensuring the covenant's enduring impact.

LOT: REMEMBRANCE AMID JUDGMENT

Lot's story begins in Genesis 11:27-31, where he is introduced as the son of Haran, Abraham's brother, making him Abraham's nephew. After Haran's death, Lot joins Abraham's migration from Ur to Canaan, sharing in the journey prompted by God's call (Genesis 12:4). By Genesis 13, their flocks grow so large that they must part ways to avoid conflict. Lot chooses the fertile Jordan Valley, settling near Sodom, a city later revealed as wicked (Genesis 13:10-13). Despite this choice, Lot remains tied to Abraham's covenantal sphere, a connection that proves lifesaving.

Genesis 18 sets the stage for Lot's deliverance. God informs Abraham of Sodom and Gomorrah's impending judgment due to their grievous sin (Genesis 18:20-21). Abraham, embodying the covenantal friendship that allows bold intercession, pleads for the cities to be spared if righteous inhabitants are found, negotiating down to ten (Genesis 18:22-33). Though Sodom lacks even this small number, Abraham's intercession indirectly benefits Lot, reflecting the covenant's promise to bless through Abraham. In Genesis 19, two angels arrive in Sodom to execute judgment, hosted by Lot, who shows hospitality despite the city's hostility (Genesis 19:1-3). When the men of Sodom demand to violate the angels, Lot protects his guests, risking himself (Genesis 19:4-9). The angels intervene, blinding the mob and urging Lot to flee with his family, his wife and two daughters, as God prepares to destroy the cities with sulfur and fire (Genesis 19:12-7). They are instructed to escape to the hills without looking back, but Lot negotiates successfully for safety in Zoar, a nearby town, revealing his hesitation (Genesis 19:18-22).

The climactic moment occurs in Genesis 19:29, where God's action is explicitly tied to His covenant with Abraham. As fire rains on Sodom and Gomorrah,

> *"God destroyed the cities of the plain, that God remembered Abra-*
> *ham, and sent Lot out of the midst of the overthrow, when He over-*
> *threw the cities in which Lot had dwelt,"*

and ensured Lot's escape. This remembrance is an active fulfillment of the covenant's promise to bless Abraham's kin. Lot's deliverance is not due to his own righteousness—his choices, like lingering in Sodom or later getting drunk (Genesis 19:30-38), show flaws—but because of Abraham's covenantal relationship with God. The angels physically take Lot out, seizing him and his family to remove them to safety (Genesis 19:16), underscoring divine initiative.

RACHEL: REMEMBRANCE AND THE GIFT OF FRUITFULNESS

The story of Rachel, found in Genesis 30:22,

> *"Then God remembered Rachel, and God listened to her and opened*
> *her womb,"*

marks a deeply personal moment of divine intervention when Jacob, Abraham's grandson, was building his family. This event, centered on Rachel's struggle with barrenness, showcases how God's remembrance of the Abrahamic covenant brings blessing to a descendant, fulfilling the promise of numerous offspring and reinforcing the covenantal friendship that binds God to His people.

Rachel's story begins in Genesis 29, where she is introduced as the daughter of Laban, the niece of Rebekah (Isaac's wife). Jacob, Abraham's grandson through Isaac, meets Rachel at a well in Haran while fleeing from his brother Esau (Genesis 29:1-12). Struck by her beauty, Jacob loves her and agrees to work seven years for Laban to marry her, only to be deceived into marrying her older sister Leah first (Genesis 29:16-25). After another seven years, Jacob marries Rachel, establishing her as his beloved wife within the covenantal line (Genesis 29:28-30). As a great-granddaughter of Abraham (via Bethuel and Rebekah) and wife of Jacob, Rachel is firmly rooted in the Abrahamic covenant, which promises descendants as numerous as the stars (Genesis 15:5).

Barrenness was a source of profound shame and sorrow, particularly for a woman expected to bear heirs. Genesis 29:31-35 reveals that while Leah bears Jacob four sons, Rachel remains barren, causing her deep distress. Her pain is compounded by rivalry with Leah, who taunts her lack of fertility. In desperation, Rachel cries to Jacob,

"Give me children, or else I die!," (Genesis 30:1)

reflecting the intensity of her longing. Jacob, frustrated, responds that only God can grant children (Genesis 30:2), pointing to divine sovereignty over the covenant's fulfillment through which Rachel is covered by her marriage to Jacob.

Rachel initially seeks a solution through her maidservant Bilhah, who bears two sons, credited to Rachel as surrogate children (Genesis 30:3-8), a common practice in the era. Yet, this does not fully alleviate Rachel's anguish, as her personal barrenness persists, threatening her role in the covenantal lineage. Her plight echoes the broader Abrahamic narrative, where Sarah's infertility (Genesis 16:1) tested the promise of descendants, underscoring that God's timing and intervention are central to covenant fulfillment.

The turning point comes in Genesis 30:22-24:

"Then God remembered Rachel, and God listened to her and opened her womb. And she conceived and bore a son, and said, 'God has taken away my reproach.' So she called his name Joseph, and said, 'The Lord shall add to me another son.'"

The phrase *"God remembered"* signifies an active divine response, a purposeful intervention at the appointed time. The text notes that God *"listened to her,"* suggesting Rachel's prayers played a role in prompting this remembrance, mirroring the covenantal friendship where God hears the cries of His people.

Rachel's conception of Joseph is a direct fulfillment of the Abrahamic covenant's promise of descendants. Joseph becomes a pivotal figure in Israel's story. His eventual rise to power in Egypt (Genesis 41–47) preserves the covenant family during famine, ensuring the survival of Abraham's lineage. Rachel's exclamation, *"God has taken away my reproach,"* reflects her relief and gratitude, as barrenness was a social stigma; her joy underscores the personal impact of God's covenantal faithfulness. Naming her son Joseph (meaning "he adds"), she expresses hope for further blessing, which is later fulfilled with the birth of Benjamin (Genesis 35:18). Tragically, she died giving birth to Benjamin (Genesis 35:16-20), but her legacy lived on as Benjamin became one of the tribes of Israel. Joseph's prominence, leading to the tribes of Ephraim and Manasseh through his sons (Genesis 48:5), amplifies the covenant's reach, as these tribes become central to Israel's identity. Rachel's tomb near Bethlehem (Genesis 35:19) becomes a lasting marker, later referenced in Jeremiah 31:15 as a symbol of maternal grief, tying her story to future covenantal promises.

HANNAH: REMEMBRANCE AND THE BIRTH OF A PROPHET

The story of Hannah, found in 1 Samuel 1 captures a poignant moment of divine intervention during Israel's turbulent transition from the era of judges to the monarchy. This narrative, centered on Hannah's struggle with barrenness and her fervent prayer, demonstrates how God's remembrance of the Abrahamic covenant extends to a descendant, fulfilling the promise of descendants and blessing through the birth of Samuel, a prophet who shapes Israel's future. It underscores the covenantal friendship, as God responds to Hannah's faith, affirming His commitment to Abraham's lineage.

Like Rachel before her, Hannah faces the profound pain of barrenness, a condition carrying social stigma in ancient Israel, where motherhood was central to identity and covenantal continuity. It is noted in 1 Samuel 1:2 that Elkanah's other wife, Peninnah, has children, while Hannah has none, fueling a rivalry.

Peninnah provokes Hannah when they go to Shiloh to worship at the tabernacle, mocking her infertility to the point of tears (1 Samuel 1:6-7). Despite Elkanah's love and provision, giving Hannah a double portion of sacrificial offerings (1 Samuel 1:4-5), her anguish persists, as she longs for a child to fulfill her role and remove her reproach.

Hannah's response is one of deep faith and initiative. During an annual pilgrimage to Shiloh, she pours out her soul in prayer at the tabernacle, vowing to dedicate her son to God's service if He grants her request (1 Samuel 1:10-11). Her prayer is silent but intense, moving her lips and prompting Eli, the high priest, to mistake her for a drunkard (1 Samuel 1:12-14). Hannah clarifies her distress, describing herself as a,

"woman of sorrowful spirit,"

who has,

"poured out my soul before the Lord." (1 Samuel 1:15-16)

Eli blesses her, praying that God grants her petition (1 Samuel 1:17), and Hannah leaves with renewed peace, her face,

"no longer sad." (1 Samuel 1:18)

The pivotal moment occurs in 1 Samuel 1:19-20:

"They rose early in the morning and worshiped before the Lord, and returned and came to their house at Ramah. And Elkanah knew Hannah his wife, and the Lord remembered her. So it came to pass in the process of time that Hannah conceived and bore a son, and

called his name Samuel, saying, 'Because I have asked for him from the Lord.'"

The phrase *"the Lord remembered her"* echoes earlier covenantal moments with Rachel, signifying God's active intervention in response to Hannah's faith and prayer. This remembrance aligns with the Abrahamic Covenant's promise of descendants, as Hannah's child will advance God's purposes for Israel.

Samuel's birth marks a turning point. Hannah names him Samuel, meaning "heard by God" or "asked of God," reflecting her gratitude for answered prayer. True to her vow, she dedicates Samuel to lifelong service as a Nazirite, presenting him to Eli at Shiloh after weaning (1 Samuel 1:21-28). Her act of surrender underscores her covenantal commitment, mirroring the friendship of faith seen in Abraham's willingness to offer Isaac (Genesis 22). Samuel grows up under God's favor, becoming a prophet, priest, and judge who anoints Saul and David, pivotal figures in establishing Israel's monarchy (1 Samuel 10:1; 16:13).

EPHRAIM: REMEMBRANCE AND THE PROMISE OF RESTORATION

Ephraim's story begins with his birth in Genesis 41:50-52, where he is introduced as the second son of Joseph, Abraham's great-grandson through Isaac, Jacob, and Rachel. Born in Egypt during Joseph's rise to power, Ephraim's name, meaning "fruitful," reflects God's blessing on Joseph in the land of affliction (Genesis 41:52). The lineage is clear: Abraham begat Isaac, Isaac begat Jacob, Jacob begat Joseph, and Joseph begat Ephraim. As a great-grandson, Ephraim is a direct heir of the Abrahamic covenant, which promises numerous descendants and a nation to bless the world (Genesis 12:2-3).

Centuries later, Ephraim's descendants have become a prominent tribe, often representing the northern kingdom of Israel after the kingdom split following Solomon's reign (Jeremiah 31). The northern kingdom, comprising ten tribes, adopts Ephraim as a leading tribe due to its size and influence. However, this kingdom falls into idolatry, worshiping Baal and forming alliances with foreign powers, leading to its conquest by Assyria (2 Kings 17:5-6). When Jeremiah prophesies, Judah (the southern kingdom) faces a similar fate, with Babylon's exile looming. Jeremiah's ministry occurs in this context of national collapse, where hope seems lost for Abraham's heirs.

In Jeremiah 31:20, God remembers,

> *"Is Ephraim My dear son? Is he a pleasant child? For though I spoke against him, I earnestly remember him still; Therefore My heart yearns for him; I will surely have mercy on him, says the Lord."*

The key phrase, *"I earnestly remember him still,"* signifies God's active remembrance, not a fleeting thought but a deliberate focus on Ephraim as a covenant heir. This remembrance, set against the backdrop of Israel's rebellion and exile, triggers a divine shift from judgment to compassion, affirming the Abrahamic covenant's enduring promise.

The crisis is dire: Assyria's conquest scatters the northern tribes, leaving their cities desolate and their identity as Abraham's heirs in question. Prophetic warnings, such as Hosea's rebuke of Ephraim's idolatry (Hosea 4:17-19) and Amos's calls for repentance (Amos 5:4-6), underscore their covenant-breaking. Judah's looming exile to Babylon (2 Kings 25) mirrors this collapse, yet Jeremiah's *Book of Consolation* (Jeremiah 30-33) offers hope. God's rhetorical questions, *"Is Ephraim My dear son? Is he a pleasant child?,"* affirm Israel's covenantal status as His child, despite their rebellion. The visceral imagery of *"my heart yearns for him"* conveys God's deep emotional investment, like a parent grieving for a lost child.

God's remembrance sparks a transformative promise of mercy, unfolding in Jeremiah 31's vision of restoration. He declares,

> *"I will bring them from the north country, And gather them from the ends of the earth...A great throng shall return there."* (Jeremiah 31:8)

God promises to rebuild Israel's communities, restore joy, and make them, *"like a well-watered garden."* (Jeremiah 31:4-12)

Rachel, Ephraim's mother, weeps for her lost children, but God comforts her:

"Refrain your voice from weeping... they shall come back from the land of the enemy." (Jeremiah 31:15-16)

This restoration extends to a renewed covenantal relationship, where God's people will,

"shout for joy" and *"will rejoice in the bounty of the Lord."* (Jeremiah 31:12)

The crowning moment is the New Covenant, announced in Jeremiah 31:31-34:

"I will make a new covenant with the house of Israel and with the house of Judah... I will put My law in their minds, and write it on their hearts... For I will forgive their iniquity, and their sin I will remember no more."

Ephraim's remembrance in verse 20 foreshadows this eternal bond, where God's forgiveness transforms the covenant into an internal reality, fulfilling Abraham's promise to bless all nations (Genesis 12:3). For Christians, Ephraim's story resonates as a promise of inclusion in God's family, where we, like Ephraim, are remembered as *"dear sons"* and invited into covenantal friendship.

REMEMBRANCE IN CHRIST

Centuries after the exile, as Israel languished under Roman rule, the promise of restoration seemed a distant memory. Yet, in the quiet of a humble home, a young woman named Mary received a message that would change the course of history. The angel Gabriel announced that she would bear the Messiah, the long-awaited Savior (Luke 1:26-38). In response, Mary sang a song of praise celebrating God's faithfulness to His covenant. Within her hymn lies a profound truth: God's remembrance of His promises was about to break forth in a way no one could have imagined.

Luke 1:54 captures this moment:

> *"He has helped His servant Israel, In remembrance of His mercy."*

Here, *"His servant Israel"* refers to the nation of Israel, God's chosen people, often described as His servant in the Old Testament. For instance, in Isaiah 41:8, God declares,

> *"But you, Israel, are My servant, Jacob whom I have chosen, The descendants of Abraham My friend."*

Mary's words echo this covenant relationship. God's help is a deliberate act of mercy, fulfilling promises made to Abraham generations before. In the broader context of Luke 1, this verse shines as part of the dawn of God's redemptive plan. John the Baptist's birth prepares the way, while Jesus, growing within Mary, emerges as the fulfillment of God's covenant with His people.

This theme of remembrance crescendos in the prophecy of Zechariah, John the Baptist's father. Filled with the Holy Spirit, Zechariah lifts his voice in a hymn of praise for God's unwavering faithfulness. In Luke 1:72 (ESV), he proclaims:

"To perform the mercy promised to our fathers, and to remember His holy covenant."

This holy covenant is the sacred oath God swore to Abraham, promising land, descendants, and blessing for all nations (Genesis 12:1-3). Zechariah celebrates that God's mercy extends not only to the patriarchs of old but also to the present moment, as the covenant finds its fulfillment in the coming of Jesus. Through Christ, the seed of Abraham, God's ancient promises bloom into a redemption that embraces the world.

Together, these verses in Luke 1 weave a tapestry of God's covenant love, stretching from the dusty plains of Abraham's journey to the humble streets of Bethlehem. From the cries of slaves in Egypt to the laments of exiles in Babylon, God remembered His people, acting in mercy to deliver and restore. Now, in the fullness of time, His remembrance takes on flesh in Jesus, the Savior who embodies the promises to Abraham and ushers in the new covenant foretold by Jeremiah (Jeremiah 31:31-34). Mary and Zechariah stand as witnesses on the threshold of redemption, their songs declaring that God's covenant is not a relic of history but a living hope. In the face of Christ, the mercy of God dawns anew, illuminating a world longing for His light.

HOW CHRISTIANS REMEMBER

If God's remembrance reflects His active faithfulness to His covenant, Christians are called to respond with their own remembrance, aligning their lives with the promises of God. This reciprocal act of remembering is woven into the fabric of Christian worship and daily life, fostering gratitude, obedience, and community, and reinforcing the covenantal bond of friendship with God. Through intentional practices, believers keep the covenant alive.

Central to Christian worship are the sacraments of baptism and communion, which serve as tangible expressions of covenantal memory. Baptism marks entry into the New Covenant, recalling God's deliverance through water, as seen in the stories of Noah's ark and the Exodus (1 Peter 3:21). It signifies believers' inclusion as friends of God, welcomed into His covenantal family (John 15:15). The Eucharist, or Lord's Supper, is even more explicitly tied to remembrance. Jesus' command,

"Do this in remembrance of Me," (Luke 22:19; 1 Corinthians 11:24-25)

invites participants to reflect on His death and resurrection, the cornerstone of the New Covenant. As 1 Corinthians 11:26 declares,

"For as often as you eat this bread and drink this cup, you proclaim the Lord's death till He comes."

This act not only commemorates Christ's sacrifice but also looks forward to His return, uniting the community in shared faith and renewing individuals in their covenantal commitment.

Beyond sacraments, Christians remember the covenant through engaging with Scripture, the written record of God's promises. Deuteronomy 8:2 urges believers to,

"remember that the Lord your God led you all the way,"

a call echoed in Psalms 105 and 106, which recount God's mighty acts from Abraham to the Exodus. Regular Bible reading and meditation keep these covenant truths vibrant, anchoring believers in God's faithfulness even amidst trials. Like David, who in Psalm 63:6-7 writes,

*"When I remember you upon my bed, and meditate on you in the
watches of the night; for you have been my help, and in the shadow
of your wings I will sing for joy,"*

we are called to dwell on God's past acts.

David penned these words in the wilderness of Judah, fleeing from his son
Absalom's rebellion, a time of betrayal and danger (2 Samuel 15-18). Exiled
from Jerusalem, pursued by his own flesh and blood who sought to seize the
throne, David faced isolation in a harsh desert. Yet, lying awake at night, he
didn't succumb to despair. Instead, he deliberately recalled God's help, meditating on the covenant that sustained him. This act stirred joy and praise, not
because his circumstances were easy, but because God's presence was near. We,
too, should emulate David, making remembrance a deliberate practice, reflecting on God's faithfulness in our darkest moments to find strength and hope.

Prayer complements this, serving as a vital avenue for remembrance. Just
as Hannah and Rachel's prayers prompted divine response (1 Samuel 1:19;
Genesis 30:22), Christians approach God with confidence, knowing He
hears their petitions. The Lord's Prayer (Matthew 6:9-13) embodies covenant
themes—hallowing God's name, seeking His kingdom, and trusting His provision and forgiveness—rooting believers in the memory of God's covenantal
relationship.

Remembering the covenant is not without challenges. Scripture warns
against spiritual amnesia:

*"Take heed to yourselves, lest you forget the covenant of the Lord your
God which He made with you."* (Deuteronomy 4:23)

Trials and doubts can tempt believers to lose sight of God's promises, yet
Lamentations 3:21-23 (ESV) offers hope:

"This I call to mind, and therefore I have hope: The steadfast love of the LORD never ceases; his mercies never come to an end."

The Holy Spirit provides divine encouragement, as Jesus promised in John 14:26:

"The Helper, the Holy Spirit, whom the Father will send in My name, He will teach you all things, and bring to your remembrance all things that I said to you."

This divine aid transforms remembrance into a mission, empowering believers to live out their covenantal identity as friends of God, proclaiming His faithfulness in word and deed. Through these practices—sacramental, scriptural, prayerful, and communal—Christians actively participate in the covenant, reflecting the same faithfulness and lovingkindness God extends to them.

CHAPTER 11

GOD'S LOVINGKINDNESS

What is the true nature of God's love as revealed in the Bible? In Psalm 107:43, we are told that,

"Whoever is wise will observe these things, And they will understand the lovingkindness of the Lord."

"These things" refers to the vivid accounts of God's redemptive acts detailed throughout the Psalm, which collectively illustrate His lovingkindness as a covenantal reality that delivers, restores, and sustains His people. It's so important that we all, by revelation, come to understand God's lovingkindness. This lovingkindness is the foundation that makes total forgiveness available to every one of us, no matter the depth of our failures or the weight of our sins, washing away our guilt and opening the floodgates of God's blessings in our lives. We are blessed today not by our own merits but directly through God's lovingkindness, which bridges the vast chasm between His perfect holiness and our imperfect humanity.

Even as born-again believers, filled with the Holy Spirit and perfect in our spirits, we remain flawed in body and soul, prone to mistakes that could distance us from Him. Yet, His lovingkindness assures us that intimacy with God is possible.

Lovingkindness reveals God's true nature, His tenderness, goodness, mercy, and compassion, setting Him apart from the conditional, often harsh relationships we experience with people. God relates to us in ways our human experiences have not prepared us for. If we truly knew Him through His lovingkindness, we would not only like Him but love Him deeply, free from unhealthy fear of condemnation or rejection. This is God's unconditional, unmerited, limitless, unfailing, and unending love—a loyal love that is woven into His very character, a love that will never let go of us, no matter how far we wander.

Previously we explored the covenantal terms "friend" and "remember," uncovering the intimate bond and active devotion that mark God's relationship with us. Now, we turn to the third term, "lovingkindness," the crowning expression of God's covenantal love. These three terms combined highlight God's relational and faithful character in covenants. In our lives, we may never encounter anyone whose love for us was rooted in their character rather than our conduct. The closest example of this we may have is our parents. Human love, even at its best, tends to be measured by how well we perform or please others. But God's lovingkindness is profoundly different, flowing not from our actions but from His unchanging character. Understanding this divine love produces a faith that anchors us in His promises. As Romans 10:17 (KJV) declares,

"So then faith cometh by hearing, and hearing by the word of God;"

faith is a natural byproduct of knowing God through His Word, where His lovingkindness is revealed. This chapter will unpack this transformative truth, showing how God's lovingkindness not only draws us into intimacy with Him but also empowers us to live as His covenant people, reflecting His steadfast love to a world in need.

FOUNDATION OF GOD'S LOVINGKINDNESS

Deuteronomy 7:6-9 (KJV) sets the tone for understanding God's lovingkindness, offering a window into the covenantal basis of God's love:

> *"For thou art an holy people unto the Lord thy God: the Lord thy God hath chosen thee to be a special people unto himself, above all people that are upon the face of the earth. The Lord did not set his love upon you, nor choose you, because ye were more in number than any people; for ye were the fewest of all people: But because the Lord loved you, and because he would keep the oath which he had sworn unto your fathers, hath the Lord brought you out with a mighty hand, and redeemed you out of the house of bondmen, from the hand of Pharaoh king of Egypt. Know therefore that the Lord thy God, he is God, the faithful God, which keepeth covenant and mercy with them that love him and keep his commandments to a thousand generations."*

This passage reveals that God's love is not arbitrary or earned; it flows from His covenantal oath, a sacred promise that binds Him to His people. The context of Deuteronomy 7 is critical to grasping the weight of this promise. As Israel stands poised to enter the Promised Land, God commands them to purge it of idolatry, setting them apart as a holy nation. Yet, their special status is not due to their own merits—neither their numbers, strength, nor righteousness, for they were *"the fewest of all people."* Instead, God's love is bestowed because of the oath He swore to their fathers: Abraham, Isaac, and Jacob. His lovingkindness is the outworking of this covenant, a love extended not because of who Israel was, but because of who God is: *"the faithful God, which keepeth covenant and mercy."*

This covenantal love sets Israel apart, but its implications extend far beyond their physical lineage. Romans 6:16 affirms this,

*"Therefore it is of faith, that it might be by grace; to the end the
promise might be sure to all the seed; not to that only which is of the
law, but to that also which is of the faith of Abraham; who is the
father of us all."*

It's the faith of Abraham in your heart that makes you special in the eyes
of God, not the blood of Abraham or any other blood. God's lovingkindness
embraces all who share Abraham's faith, transcending ethnicity or status. Even
under the Mosaic Covenant of Sinai, with its rigorous laws, Deuteronomy 7
points back to the Abrahamic promise, underscoring that God's love precedes
and undergirds the Law. His lovingkindness is not contingent on Israel's performance but flows from His nature and His oath, a love that redeemed them from
Pharaoh's chains and continues to redeem us today. We are special in God's eyes
not because of our background, status, or deeds, but because of our faith in His
covenantal promises, ultimately fulfilled through Jesus Christ. God's lovingkindness flows from His faithfulness, a love that reaches out to us not because we
deserve it but because He has pledged Himself to us in an everlasting bond.

PSALM 107: GOD'S LOVINGKINDNESS

Psalm 107 serves as a magnificent hymn of praise, celebrating God's unwavering
mercy and deliverance in a way that profoundly illustrates His covenantal lovingkindness toward His people. Composed likely during the post-exilic period,
after Israel's return from Babylonian captivity around the 6th century BC, this
psalm reflects on the nation's history of rebellion, suffering, and restoration.
While some commentators view it as a general assertion of God's providence over
all humanity, its imagery draws heavily from Israel's experiences—wandering in
the wilderness, captivity, and storms of life—echoing the covenantal promises
made to Abraham and reaffirmed at Sinai. The psalm's purpose is to call the
redeemed to give thanks, highlighting how God's lovingkindness responds to
human cries with redemption, not as a reward for merit but as a fulfillment of His

faithful bond. Its structure is particularly striking, featuring two key statements repeated four times each, a pattern unparalleled elsewhere in Scripture, emphasizing the reliability of God's lovingkindness in the face of distress.

The psalm opens with a resounding call to gratitude:

> *"Oh give thanks to the Lord, for He is good! For His mercy endures forever."* (v.1)

This sets the tone for a series of vignettes that showcase God's deliverance, each building on the covenantal theme of mercy triumphing over judgment. The first repeated statement appears in verses 6, 13, 19, and 28:

> *"Then they cried out to the Lord in their trouble, and He delivered them out of their distresses."*

This refrain captures the essence of God's compassionate response, even under the covenant of Sinai, where His wrath was revealed against disobedience through curses outlined in Deuteronomy 28. At Sinai, God established a framework where rebellion invited divine discipline, yet His lovingkindness ensured that a sincere cry for help brought swift forgiveness and restoration. If Israel strayed and began reaping the consequences of their actions, such as famine, oppression, or exile, a simple plea triggered His mercy. This pattern reveals a God who, though holy and just, does not relish punishment; He desires repentance and renewal, forgiving instantly when His people turn to Him.

Consider the implications of this mercy in everyday terms. Humans often withhold forgiveness, nursing grudges that linger long after apologies are made. We've all experienced it: wronging a friend or loved one, seeking pardon, only to find that while they may say they've forgiven us, their demeanor changes. They treat us differently, taking months or even years to warm back up. God's lovingkindness operates on an entirely different level. It is a covenantal love that doesn't hold our failures against us. He doesn't want us to suffer, even when we've brought hardship upon ourselves through poor choices. Many of our troubles stem from our own decisions, yet God yearns to forgive, restore, cleanse, and shower us with His tender mercies, thwarting the enemy's plans in the process. When we falter, our instincts, fueled by guilt, embarrassment, or shame, may drive us to hide from God, much like Adam and Eve in the garden. We feel we must earn our way back, performing acts of penance to regain His favor. But this mindset is a deception, skillfully sown by Satan to distance us from our Father.

The truth is, through faith in the blood covenant sealed by Jesus, we are made the very righteousness of God (2 Corinthians 5:21). This righteousness isn't based on our flawless conduct but on His covenantal promise, where God declares He will be merciful to our unrighteousness and remember our sins no more. Salvation often brings quick changes to outward behaviors visible to others. But the deeper transformations of heart attitudes, lingering unbelief, or hidden struggles take time. During this process, we may feel condemned, knowing better yet falling short. Satan exploits this guilt, convincing us that God keeps a ledger of our mistakes, driving countless believers away from intimacy with Him and hindering their calling. How many have sat in church for decades, letting dreams and ministries fade because of a major stumble, believing God holds it against them forever? Yet, Romans 4 reveals the blessedness Abraham and David experienced: the joy of being made right with God apart from works, a righteousness credited through faith alone. This understanding is vital to our future, it frees us to approach God boldly, knowing His lovingkindness preserves us, not our perfection.

Complementing this cry-and-deliverance motif is the psalm's second repeated statement, found in verses 8, 15, 21, and 31:

> *"Oh, that men would give thanks to the Lord for His goodness, and for His wonderful works to the children of men!"*

This fourfold repetition follows each vignette of distress and deliverance, underscoring that God's lovingkindness is not a distant attribute but a living reality that evokes gratitude. Verse 8 comes after the first vignette (verses 4-7), where wanderers lost in the desert cry out in their thirst and hunger, and God guides them to a city of safety. This mirrors Israel's wilderness experience under the Mosaic covenant, where God's lovingkindness provided manna and water despite their grumbling (Exodus 16-17). The call to praise in verse 8 emphasizes that His lovingkindness is displayed in these "wonderful works," acts of provision that sustain life. Giving thanks here is not rote ritual but a recognition that God's covenantal love turns desperation into abundance, fostering a gratitude that acknowledges our dependence on Him, much like a child trusting a parent's ca re.

Verse 15 follows the second story (verses 10-14), depicting prisoners in chains, afflicted by their own rebellion against God's word, who are freed when they cry out. This echoes the Babylonian exile, a consequence of covenant unfaithfulness (2 Kings 25), yet God's lovingkindness shatters their bonds, breaking iron bars as a sign of His mercy. The refrain urges praise for His goodness, reminding us that lovingkindness redeems even the self-inflicted wounds of sin. Thanksgiving in this context becomes a covenantal affirmation: by praising His wonderful works, we honor the God who preserves us through discipline, turning judgment into restoration and inviting us to live in renewed obedience.

Verse 21 appears after the third narrative (verses 17-20), where fools sickened by iniquity near death's gates are healed by God's word upon their cry. Drawing from Israel's cycles of idolatry and affliction (Judges 2-3), this highlights how God's lovingkindness intervenes in spiritual sickness, offering healing as a covenantal promise (Exodus 15:26). The call to praise celebrates His goodness, transforming gratitude into a weapon against despair. It teaches that lovingkindness is not permissive but redemptive, stirring thanks that motivates us to forsake sin and embrace His faithfulness.

Finally, verse 31 concludes the fourth vignette (verses 23-30), where sailors tossed by storms cry out, and God calms the seas, guiding them to harbor. Evoking Jonah's storm (Jonah 1) or broader covenantal sovereignty over creation (Genesis 8:22), this shows God's lovingkindness extending beyond Israel to all humanity. The refrain's plea for praise culminates the psalm, linking all deliverances to God's wonderful works. Together, these verses reveal that giving thanks for His lovingkindness is a covenantal act—acknowledging that His mercy preserves us, turns trials into testimonies, and draws us into deeper intimacy, reflecting the relational bond where His goodness evokes our eternal gratitude.

GOD SHOWS DAVID LOVINGKINDNESS

The life of David is absolutely incredible, showcasing triumph, failure, and divine grace that reveals the overwhelming lovingkindness of God. David was a great king, a man after God's own heart, yet he committed some truly egregious sins. Despite these missteps, he wound up being the greatest king Israel ever had, embodying a wealth of wisdom through his experiences with God and the workings of His kingdom. Nowhere is this more evident than in the events of 2 Samuel 11 and 12, where David's grievous mistakes collide with God's steadfast covenantal love, ultimately leading to his restoration. This narrative showcases a God whose mercy not only forgives but redeems, turning even the darkest moments into opportunities for grace.

It was the season when kings traditionally went out to war, a time when David, as the leader of Israel, should have been at the forefront of battle. Instead, he sent his army out under Joab's command and remained in Jerusalem. One afternoon, David rose from his bed and wandered onto the terrace of his palace. From there, he caught sight of Bathsheba, a beautiful woman bathing. Lust ignited within him as he gazed upon her, and rather than turning away, he allowed temptation to take root. He summoned her to the palace, and though Bathsheba's complicity in the affair was wrong, the cultural dynamics of the time made it nearly impossible for her to refuse the king without risking severe consequences, perhaps even death. This does not absolve her, but it highlights the difficult position she faced. David and Bathsheba slept together, and soon after, she sent word to him that she was pregnant.

What began as a lustful glance quickly spiraled into a web of sin. David had lusted in his heart, committed adultery, and now sought to conceal his actions. His first attempt at a cover-up was to bring Bathsheba's husband, Uriah, back from the battlefield. Uriah was one of David's mighty men of valor, an elite group of 37 warriors listed in 2 Samuel 23:8-39, known for their exceptional bravery and loyalty. These were not men who earned their place through politics but through proven courage and devotion to David and Israel. David urged Uriah to go home and spend the night with his wife, hoping that if Uriah slept with Bathsheba, the pregnancy could be attributed to him, and no one would suspect the king's involvement. But Uriah, a man of unshakable integrity, refused. He told David it wouldn't feel right to enjoy the comforts of home while his fellow soldiers endured the hardships of war, separated from their families.

Undeterred, David tried a second tactic: he wined and dined Uriah, getting him drunk in the hopes that intoxication would lower his resolve. Yet even in that state, Uriah's loyalty held firm, he still would not go home. Desperate and cornered, David resorted to a chilling plan. He wrote a letter to Joab, instructing him to place Uriah at the forefront of a fierce battle and then retreat, ensuring Uriah's death. Joab followed the king's orders, and Uriah, a loyal friend who had laid down his life for David in countless battles, was killed. This was no casualty of war; it was murder, orchestrated by the king who should have protected him. David's heart had hardened, his conscience seared as if with a hot iron, and God was deeply displeased.

But God's lovingkindness does not abandon His people, even in their darkest moments. He sent Nathan, the prophet, to confront David. In 2 Samuel 12:1-4, Nathan entered the king's presence and began with a story:

> "There were two men in one city, one rich and the other poor. The rich man had exceedingly many flocks and herds. But the poor man had nothing, except one little ewe lamb which he had bought and nourished; and it grew up together with him and with his children. It ate of his own food and drank from his own cup and lay in his

*bosom; and it was like a daughter to him. And a traveler came
to the rich man, who refused to take from his own flock and from
his own herd to prepare one for the wayfaring man who had come
to him; but he took the poor man's lamb and prepared it for the
man who had come to him."*

David, incensed by the injustice, slammed his fist on the table and declared
in 2 Samuel 12:5-7:

*"'As the Lord lives, the man who has done this shall surely die!
And he shall restore fourfold for the lamb, because he did this
thing and because he had no pity.' Then Nathan said to David,
'You are the man!'"*

The weight of those words shattered David's defenses. He, the king with
multiple wives and boundless resources, had taken Bathsheba, the wife of his
loyal friend, and then arranged Uriah's death to cover it up. Nathan revealed
God's displeasure, not just with the acts of adultery and murder, but with
the betrayal of trust and abuse of power. What set David apart, however, was
his response. Unlike many who might have deflected blame or hardened their
hearts further, David was shaken to his core. He immediately recognized that
his sin was not only against Bathsheba and Uriah but ultimately against God Hi
mself.

"I have sinned against the Lord,"

he confessed (2 Samuel 12:13), and in that moment of repentance, the
lovingkindness of God began to flow into his life.

God's mercy was immediate. Nathan assured David,

"The Lord also has put away your sin; you shall not die." (2 Samuel 12:13)

According to the Mosaic Law in place during David's time, his actions warranted the death penalty: Leviticus 20:10 prescribes death for adultery, and Numbers 35:16-21 mandates the same for murder. Despite the gravity of David's sins and the legal consequences he deserved as king, God chose to show him mercy through His extraordinary lovingkindness. Yet sin, even when forgiven, often leaves ripples of consequence. The child born from David's affair with Bathsheba fell gravely ill. David interceded desperately, fasting and lying on the ground, pleading for the baby's life. Despite his prayers, the child died, a heartbreaking outcome that reflected the gravity of David's actions. Bathsheba's heart was broken, and David, too, mourned deeply. Yet when the child passed, David rose, washed himself, and worshiped God, demonstrating a trust in God's sovereignty even amid loss.

God's lovingkindness, however, did not stop at forgiveness, it extended to restoration. David comforted Bathsheba, and they conceived again. This time, she bore a son named Solomon, and the Scriptures note that,

"the Lord loved him." (2 Samuel 12:24)

God even sent Nathan to give the child a second name (covenant ritual 4), Jedidiah, meaning "beloved of the Lord." Solomon would grow to be another of Israel's greatest kings, renowned for his wisdom, and more importantly, he would become a key figure in the lineage of Jesus, the Messiah. Through the genealogy of Christ, we see that God not only forgave David and Bathsheba but wove their story into His redemptive plan for humanity.

This is the breathtaking scope of God's lovingkindness, it doesn't just pardon; it redeems and restores. David's sins were unimaginable: lust, adultery, deceit, and the murder of a faithful friend. Yet God's mercy was greater still. He didn't cast David aside or nullify His covenant; instead, He brought forth beauty from brokenness. The relationship that began in sin, once transformed by repentance, became a conduit for God's purposes. Solomon's birth and his role in the lineage of Jesus stand as enduring testaments to the fact that God can take even our gravest mistakes and, through repentance, turn them into something godly and glorious.

David's story offers profound wisdom for us today. If God could forgive David for such hideous acts, He can forgive anyone for anything they've done. If He could restore David and Bathsheba, taking a union birthed in ungodliness and bringing forth a king who would contribute to the Messiah's lineage, then He can bring great things out of our lives as well, because of our repentance. David didn't excuse his sin or shift blame; he owned it fully and sought God's mercy. In response, God not only forgave but restored him to a place of purpose and honor within His covenantal plan.

The lovingkindness of God in David's life is beyond imagination, a wild and beautiful dream of grace. It reveals a God who doesn't just tolerate us in our failures but loves us with an everlasting love, calling us back to Him no matter how far we've strayed. David's experience teaches us that no one is beyond the reach of God's mercy. When we turn to Him in genuine repentance, His lovingkindness meets us, forgives us, and sets us on a path of restoration. Through David, we see that God's covenantal relationship is not fragile—it endures our mistakes, and through His unfathomable grace, it fulfills His promises, bringing the Messiah into the world and offering hope to all who seek Him.

LIVING OUT GOD'S LOVINGKINDNESS

God's steadfast, covenantal lovingkindness is not just a gift to receive, it is a calling to embody. We are called to mirror the lovingkindness we've received, relating to others with the same grace, mercy, and tenderness that God extends to us. As Psalm 40:11 pleads,

"Do not withhold Your tender mercies from me, O Lord; Let Your lovingkindness and Your truth continually preserve me,"

we see that God's lovingkindness is our preservation, a shield against Satan's schemes to draw us away through guilt and condemnation. This same love equips us to transform lives around us, reflecting the heart of our covenant-keeping God. When we preach God's judgment and righteousness apart from His lovingkindness, we risk pushing people away from Him, painting a distorted picture of a wrathful deity rather than the compassionate Father revealed in Christ.

Understanding lovingkindness reshapes our relationship with God and others in profound ways. First, it inspires gratitude and worship. Psalm 107:8 (ESV) urges,

"Let them thank the Lord for his steadfast love, for his wondrous works."

When we grasp how good God has been, saving us, healing us, speaking to us despite our unworthiness, praise becomes unstoppable. Struggles with worship and thanksgiving fade when we grasp how good God has been, shifting focus from our flaws to His faithfulness.

Second, it fosters trust and security. This trust in God's lovingkindness is not meant to be hoarded but shared, shaping how we approach others in our daily lives. Just as God's lovingkindness meets us in our brokenness, we are called to extend this same steadfast love to those around us. To reflect lovingkindness is to offer forgiveness without keeping score, to show kindness without expecting repayment, and to love with a patience that mirrors God's own. When someone hurts us, human instinct may urge us to withdraw or demand justice, but lovingkindness calls us to pursue reconciliation, just as God pursues us. This means listening to a struggling neighbor without judgment, extending grace to a coworker who falters, or offering compassion to someone trapped in sin, even when it's inconvenient. In a world where relationships are often transactional, reflecting lovingkindness requires us to break that cycle, choosing to love others not because they deserve it, but because we have been loved first by a God whose lovingkindness never fails.

Third, it empowers forgiveness and reconciliation. Experiencing God's mercy compels us to extend grace as freely as God does, even to those who've wronged us, breaking the cycle of human grudges. Ephesians 4:32 instructs,

> *"Be kind to one another, tenderhearted, forgiving one another, even as God in Christ forgave you."*

This verse reflects the heart of lovingkindness, a love that forgives not because it is earned, but because it flows from God's merciful nature. Human grudges linger, months to warm up after betrayal, but God's instant forgiveness models a better way. Lovingkindness calls us to forgive swiftly and fully, as God does. This might mean reconciling with a friend who betrayed us, choosing to release their offense rather than harboring bitterness, just as God releases our sins through the blood of Christ (Colossians 1:14). It could involve extending grace to a family member who has wounded us, welcoming them back with a warm embrace rather than a cold shoulder. It means reaching out to a coworker who has slandered us, offering kind words instead of retaliation, knowing that lovingkindness seeks restoration over revenge. Lovingkindness frees us from bitterness, mirroring His tender mercies to others.

Fourth, it motivates holiness, not as a burden but as a response to a love that calls us to reflect His character. God's lovingkindness is not a license to sin; it calls us higher. Romans 2:4 notes,

> *"The goodness of God leads you to repentance."*

Seeing Christ's sacrifice stirs a desire to honor Him, not exploit His grace. It's a love that preserves us, giving time to align with His will, as David prays in Psalm 51:1,

"Have mercy upon me, O God, According to Your lovingkindness."

David's cry is not for an indulgence to continue sinning but for mercy to be restored, transformed by a love that forgives and preserves. God's lovingkindness gives us time to grow, to align our lives with His holiness, not because we fear punishment but because His lovingkindness awakens a longing to honor Him.

Fifth, God's lovingkindness cultivates a deep wellspring of compassion within us, compelling us to extend this same lovingkindness to others in practical, selfless ways that mirror His heart. Jesus sets the standard in John 13:34:

> *"A new commandment I give to you, that you love one another; as I have loved you, that you also love one another."*

This command is not a suggestion but a covenantal call to reflect the lovingkindness we have received, a love that is sacrificial, unconditional, and relentless. Even when faced with hostility, lovingkindness calls us to pray for those who oppose us, as Jesus instructs in Matthew 5:44:

> *"Love your enemies, bless those who curse you."*

In a culture where compassion is often reserved for the "deserving," reflecting lovingkindness is radically countercultural, requiring us to set aside pride, self-interest, and the temptation to judge. By loving others as God loves us, without conditions or expectations, we become ambassadors of His covenantal love, fostering communities where compassion heals wounds and draws others to the God whose lovingkindness never fails.

As Christians, we are not just recipients of this love but ambassadors of it. To show lovingkindness is to live out our covenant with God, extending His mercy to a world desperate for hope. When we forgive the unforgivable, love the unlovely, and serve without expecting return, we embody the lovingkindness that defines God's heart. This is no easy task, it requires us to set aside pride, judgment, and the temptation to demand justice over mercy. Yet, as we've seen with David, God's lovingkindness meets us in our mess and invites us to do the same for others. We must renew our hearts to know God's lovingkindness deeply, to let it ignite our worship and steady our faith, and to share it generously, drawing others not to a God of wrath, but to the One whose love never lets go. In doing so, we fulfill the covenantal call to be His people, reflecting His lovingkindness in a world that so desperately needs it.

REVEALING THE
SECRET

We've covered many biblical accounts of covenants and how God has blessed those He is in covenant with. We too can be blessed under the New Covenant but how do we reveal the secret of the Lord to work in our lives? How do we go from seeing His miracles and blessings work for others to having these blessings and miracles work in our lives too? The final three chapters will discuss how we should approach God and gain an understanding of His ways. As you learn to fear and depend on God, your faith will grow and His secret will be revealed to you.□

Reveal the secret by:

1 – FEARING GOD
2 – DEPENDING ON GOD
3 – FAITH IN GOD

FEARING GOD

As we have journeyed through the profound depths of God's covenant language, we now turn our focus to the theme that undergirds them all: the fear of the Lord. This reverential awe serves as the gateway to understanding His covenants and revealing the secret of the Lord. We will confront the pitfalls of fearing man and the distortions of religious fear, which bind us through man-made doctrines and unhealthy dread; explore our departure from the law's shadow of wrath, embracing the grace of the New Covenant; learn how to fear God rightly through the Spirit and the Word, following the example of Jesus; stand in awe of His majesty, where reverence inspires holiness and departure from evil; and discover how this godly fear supernaturally produces repentance, a transformative change that aligns our lives with His kingdom purposes. Through these explorations, we will see how true fear of the Lord liberates us from bondage, draws us into intimacy with God, and equips us to live out the blessings of His eternal covenants.

THE FEAR OF MAN

Before we delve into the beauty of Godly fear, we must confront its counterfeit: the fear of man, often cloaked in religious garb. This unhealthy fear distorts our view of God, binding us in chains of doubt and condemnation, and keeps us from revealing the secret of the Lord. This ungodly fear keeps people bound in their circumstances. This is not the awe-inspired reverence Scripture calls us to, but a tormenting dread that paralyzes the soul. It manifests as the fear of failing God, where every misstep feels like an irreparable breach in the relationship. People gripped by this fear live in constant anxiety, believing that one wrong choice will invoke divine wrath. They worry that making a mistake means God is going to punish them, perhaps with hardship or loss, turning their walk with Him into a minefield rather than a journey of grace. Even worse, some harbor the fear that God is going to do a bad thing to them, even in obedience, as if following Him invites calamity rather than blessing.

Many live under this religious fear, bound by condemnation, guilt, and shame from the past, which locks them into bondage. This fear whispers that their sins are too great, their failures too many, for God to truly forgive or use them. It echoes the accusations of the enemy, keeping believers trapped in cycles of self-doubt and spiritual stagnation. Yet Scripture assures us that we have been delivered from this very fear. Through Christ, we are freed to serve God without this crippling dread, stepping into a relationship marked by boldness and peace.

Beyond religious fear lies a demonic fear that holds so many people down, a literal spirit of fear that seeks to undermine faith. The world is filled with this fear, which evolves into worry, stress, and anxiety—burdens God does not want His people to carry. In 2 Timothy 1:7, Paul reminds us,

"For God has not given us a spirit of fear, but of power and of love and of a sound mind."

This verse exposes fear as something foreign to God's design, a tool of the adversary that robs us of the authority, affection, and clarity He provides. Instead of living in torment, we are equipped to face life with divine strength. Proverbs 29:25 captures another facet of this unhealthy fear:

"The fear of man brings a snare, But whoever trusts in the Lord shall be safe."

The fear of man is a snare that traps us, preventing us from stepping into God's purposes. We fear that if we change and pursue His calling, our families will reject us, or our peers will turn away. What are people going to think of us? What will they say if we start speaking in other tongues or boldly sharing our faith? This fear keeps us bound, prioritizing human approval over divine obedience. It silences our witness and stifles our growth, turning potential into paralysis.

Jesus addresses this directly in Matthew 10:27-28, saying,

> *"Whatever I tell you in the dark, speak in the light; and what you hear in the ear, preach on the housetops. And do not fear those who kill the body but cannot kill the soul. But rather fear Him who is able to destroy both soul and body in hell."*

He instructs us not to fear what man can do to us or what man thinks of us, but to fear Him who holds eternal authority. Once we start to fear God properly, understanding it as reverential awe, it delivers us from the fear of man. The worst thing man can do to us is kill us. Yet God says not to fear those who can only harm the body, but to fear Him who can affect both body and soul in hell.

There is a healthy fear that delivers us from unhealthy fear. Walking in the fear of God supernaturally frees us from the tormenting snare of fearing man, what he says, what he thinks, and what he can do to us. Multitudes are held down by this, missing out on God's freedom because they prioritize human opinion over divine truth. In John 12:42-43, we see this played out:

> *"Nevertheless even among the rulers many believed in Him, but because of the Pharisees they did not confess Him, lest they should be put out of the synagogue; for they loved the praise of men more than the praise of God."*

They feared rejection from the religious community of their day, and John reveals the heart of their problem: they loved the praise of men more than the praise of God.

One of the reasons we get hooked on the praise of men is that we don't know God praises us. In our covenant relationship with Him, secured through the sacrifice of Jesus, God delights in us and affirms us as His children. The fear of the Lord is a powerful force working in our hearts and lives, equipping us to bear anything from man. Honoring God is a part of fearing Him, and when we honor men rather than God, it leads to our own demise. Romans 13:7 instructs,

> *"Render therefore to all their due: taxes to whom taxes are due, customs to whom customs, fear to whom fear, honor to whom honor."*

There are some things we are to fear, and that is God. When we fear Him, we will not fear what man can do to us.

Psalm 34:1-2 declares,

> *"I will bless the Lord at all times; His praise shall continually be in my mouth. My soul shall make its boast in the Lord; The humble shall hear of it and be glad."*

When we make our boast in God, the humble hear it and are glad. It is the prideful who hear it and get mad; it is the religious people who hear it and get mad. This reveals the divide: true humility rejoices in God's praise, while pride resists it.

Isaiah 29:13 exposes the root of religious fear:

> *"Therefore the Lord said: 'Inasmuch as these people draw near with their mouths And honor Me with their lips, But have removed their hearts far from Me, And their fear toward Me is taught by the commandment of men.'"*

Notice what happens when men teach religious fear to the people: it pushes them away from God. They still honor Him with their lips, but their hearts are far removed from Him. The thing that drives people away from God is not demonic fear alone; it is an unhealthy fear of God, a religious fear born of false doctrine. This includes tormenting ideas like, if you don't tithe, God is going to make you pay for it in doctor bills; if you don't serve Him and live holy, God is going to bring cancer to you. All this religious fear, taught by the precepts of men, has caused people to back up from God. It's this same religious fear that put Jesus on the cross.

What person on this earth would you get close to if you knew that, if you messed up somehow, they were going to bring sickness on you or financial ruin? You could never be intimate with anyone if that is what could happen. But that is how some people think of God. We don't need the fear of man, but the fear of God in an awestruck way. Matthew 15:7-9 quotes Isaiah, saying,

> *"Hypocrites! Well did Isaiah prophesy about you, saying: 'These people draw near to Me with their mouth, And honor Me with their lips, But their heart is far from Me. And in vain they worship Me, Teaching as doctrines the commandments of men.'"*

Jesus calls them hypocrites, noting that they say one thing with their mouths and honor God with their lips, but their hearts are far from Him, and they worship in vain because they have been taught the doctrines of men in place of the doctrine of God. They have been taught what man said God was and how God was, versus what God said He was and how He was.

Romans 8:15 affirms,

> *"For you did not receive the spirit of bondage again to fear, but you received the Spirit of adoption by whom we cry out, 'Abba, Father.'"*

Paul says we did not receive the spirit of bondage again to fear. Fear brings us into bondage, the fear of man. No matter what fear we have, somewhere a man taught us an unhealthy fear. We have to be careful when raising our kids; they are fearless, and because we don't understand the fear of the Lord, the healthy, wholesome fear, we use negative fear to constrain our children many times, producing an unhealthy fear for things in their life.

Psalm 34:11 invites,

"Come, you children, listen to me; I will teach you the fear of the Lord."

We are taught the fear of God; God teaches us to fear Him. When man teaches fearing God, it is usually his commandments, traditions, and precepts, and it pushes people away from God. God, by His Spirit and His Word, will teach us His fear if we will truly love Him back as He has loved us.

DEPARTING FROM THE LAW

Much of the religious fear that still grips Christians today finds its roots in the Old Testament at Sinai, where the law was given amid thunder and fire. Yet, many believers do not fully grasp that we are under a New Covenant with God, one of grace and intimacy rather than rigid commandments and curses. This misunderstanding perpetuates a fear that binds rather than frees.

Paul writes in 2 Corinthians 7:1,

"Therefore, having these promises, beloved, let us cleanse ourselves from all filthiness of the flesh and spirit, perfecting holiness in the fear of God."

Notice that holiness is perfected not in the law, nor in punishment, curses, or wrath, but in the fear of God, a reverential awe that draws us into His purifying presence. This stands in sharp contrast to the religious fear that plagues many, which stems from a misapplication of the Old Testament law. In Romans 2:4, Paul asks,

> *"Or do you despise the riches of His goodness, forbearance, and long-suffering, not knowing that the goodness of God leads you to repentance?"*

It is God's lovingkindness, not His severity under the law, that softens our hearts and leads us to turn toward Him.

If the law could make a man righteous, and if living under the law could produce true intimacy with God, why did God not give the law to Adam and Eve in the garden? Why did He not reveal it to Enoch, who walked with Him so closely that he disappeared without tasting death? Why was it not given to Noah, a righteous man in a corrupt generation, whom God chose to preserve humanity through the flood? If God was ever going to bestow the law to foster righteousness and closeness, surely He would have given it to Noah, but He did not. Why did He withhold it from Abraham, the father of faith, or from Isaac and Jacob, or even from the twelve tribes and Joseph in Egypt?

God had a specific purpose for the law during a particular season, and it was not to reveal His heart in intimacy. Instead, the law serves to reveal sin, as Romans 3:20 states:

> *"Therefore by the deeds of the law no flesh will be justified in His sight, for by the law is the knowledge of sin."*

It was not designed to make anyone righteous but to show humanity that we are not righteous on our own. The law does not produce faith; rather, it drives us to faith, stripping away self-confidence so that we call upon the name of the Lord for salvation. As Galatians 3:24 explains,

"Therefore the law was our tutor to bring us to Christ, that we might be justified by faith."

Under the Old Covenant at Sinai, the law acted as a mirror, reflecting our inadequacy and pointing us toward the need for a Savior who would fulfill its demands.

This is why Paul declares in Galatians 3:13-14,

"Christ has redeemed us from the curse of the law, having become a curse for us (for it is written, 'Cursed is everyone who hangs on a tree'), that the blessing of Abraham might come upon the Gentiles in Christ Jesus, that we might receive the promise of the Spirit through faith."

Through Christ's sacrifice, the blessing of Abraham rests on us and our families, and we are no longer under a curse. God will never curse us, never punish us in wrath, and never be angry with us again, for we have been delivered from the wrath that is to come. There is indeed a wrath of God, and there is a hell, prepared not for people but for the devil and his angels, as Matthew 25:41 affirms:

"Then He will also say to those on the left hand, 'Depart from Me, you cursed, into the everlasting fire prepared for the devil and his angels.'"

God does not want anyone to go there. But, He sent Jesus so that if we call upon the name of the Lord, we will be saved. God desires that all be saved, as 2 Peter 3:9 states:

"The Lord is not slack concerning His promise, as some count slackness, but is longsuffering toward us, not willing that any should perish but that all should come to repentance."

Yet, He gives us the choice to love Him back. He loves us unconditionally, but He will not force us to reciprocate; that free will and free choice remain profound throughout our entire lives. We must choose to fear God properly, in awe and reverence, to see the benefits and fruit of that fear. Under the New Covenant, we are invited into a relationship where His Spirit dwells within us, empowering us to live holy lives not out of dread of curses but out of gratitude for His grace. This departure from the law frees us from religious fear, allowing us to approach God as beloved children, perfected in holiness through the fear that honors His goodness and draws us ever closer to His heart.

HOW TO FEAR GOD

Having departed from the law's shadow of wrath and curses, embracing instead the New Covenant's grace that redeems us and bestows Abraham's blessings, we now explore the practical path to fearing God rightly. This godly fear is not innate or accidental; it is cultivated through the Spirit and the Word, transforming our lives from the inside out. People who fear God have the Spirit of the fear of the Lord in them. That is the beginning of wisdom and the beginning of understanding as Proverbs 9:10 declares,

"The fear of the Lord is the beginning of wisdom, And the knowledge of the Holy One is understanding."

The minute you do fear God in your heart, it is so powerful what begins to happen in your life, wisdom flows, decisions align with His will, and intimacy deepens.

Psalm 128:1 promises,

"Blessed is every one who fears the Lord, Who walks in His ways."

Notice that the fearing of God comes first before the walking in His ways. Reverence precedes obedience, laying the foundation for a blessed life. Hebrews 12:28 exhorts,

> *"Therefore, since we are receiving a kingdom which cannot be shaken, let us have grace, by which we may serve God acceptably with reverence and godly fear."*

There is a godly fear versus a demonic fear, a good kind of fear versus a negative, bad kind of fear. John 4:24 states,

> *"God is Spirit, and those who worship Him must worship in spirit and truth."*

So there is a fearing of God in spirit and in truth that is very productive, very profound in a New Testament believer's life. Yet most of us have either been taught an improper fear of God or no fear of God at all. Many were taught a religious fear or a tormenting fear of God that drives them away from Him instead of closer to Him. God wants to reverse that in our lives so He can reveal the secret to us.

God wants to take us out of the religious fear we are in, into a healthy, wholesome fear of Him. To fear God is to reverence God; to have a reverence for God is to have a deep-seated respect for God. Respect for God, to fear God, is to honor God. This truth unfolds vividly at Mount Sinai in Exodus 20:18-19:

> *"Now all the people witnessed the thunderings, the lightning flashes, the sound of the trumpet, and the mountain smoking; and when the*

*people saw it, they trembled and stood afar off. Then they said to
Moses, 'You speak with us, and we will hear; but let not God speak
with us, lest we die.'"*

This is when God delivered the children of Israel out of Egypt and brought
them unto Himself. God never delivers us out of anything into nothing. God
always delivers us out of something to take us into something else. He delivered
the children of Israel out of Egypt, not just to escape bondage, but into the
kingdom of God. The Bible says God has delivered us from the power of darkness
and translated us into the kingdom of His dear Son, the kingdom of light. So God
did not save you to have you saved and stuck. God saved you to take you into His
divine purpose for your life and destiny now.

The Israelites did not understand that God saved and delivered them out of
something into Himself and for His good pleasure. They were at Mount Sinai,
where God gave them the Ten Commandments. This mountain was on fire with
smoke bellowing from it. There was thunder and lightning. We have to remember
that the Israelites were not born again like we are born again. They were not filled
with the Holy Spirit like we are filled with the Holy Spirit. They did not have
a Bible. They did not know who they were or who their God was. They were
in bondage and slavery for over 400 years and now God shows up, and they are
shaking. The mountain is smoking, and when the people saw it, they stood afar
off and said unto Moses, "Speak with us, and we will hear. But don't let God
speak to us or we'll die." This is like saying, "Pastor, we don't want to hear what
God is saying. You go hear what God is saying and come back and tell us what
God is saying."

That was the biggest mistake the Israelites made in their entire history, is not
wanting to hear God themselves. Does this sound familiar today? Thousands of
years later, churches are filled with people who do not want to hear God for
themselves. They want the pastor to fast and pray, to be disciplined, and to live a
sanctified life. Then every Sunday the pastor can tell them what God is saying. A
pastor's job is to affirm what God has been saying to you in your hearts and in your

lives. A pastor is supposed to be a blessing to you, of encouragement. A pastor is not supposed to replace the voice of God in your life. There is not supposed to be mediators between you and God. God has removed the mediation between you and Him through the blood of His Son so that you can have access to God and fear Him with a godly fear.

Exodus 20:20 continues,

> *"And Moses said to the people, 'Do not fear; for God has come to test you, and that His fear may be before you, so that you may not sin.'"*

Every time God would show up, the first thing He would say is "Do not fear." Why did God have to say to them constantly, "Do not fear"? Because they were afraid. They had an ungodly fear that was taught by man. God came to test us so we could have His fear before our face to help us to stop sinning. Moses understood how to fear God and drew near to Him. The Israelites may have said it with their mouth, but it wasn't in their hearts. God is testing us, do not be afraid.

Think of any fear you currently have and try to trace it back to its origin. Most likely you will find that somebody taught you that fear. Once you begin to really see the goodness of God, you do not want to displease Him and live in sin. You want to be holy, and that is what the fear of the Lord does. Deuteronomy 4:9-10 instructs,

> *"Only take heed to yourself, and diligently keep yourself, lest you forget the things your eyes have seen, and lest they depart from your heart all the days of your life. And teach them to your children and your grandchildren, especially concerning the day you stood before the Lord your God in Horeb, when the Lord said to me, 'Gather the people to Me, and I will let them hear My words, that they may learn to fear Me all the days they live on the earth, and that they may teach their children.'"*

We learn to fear God by learning His word. Then we have to teach our children how to fear God. They will not fear God automatically or even just by participating at church. They have to be taught the word of God. It's the word of God that teaches us what is good and bad, what is moral and immoral, what is light and what is dark. If we do not learn to fear God, we will not depart from evil. We will stay in darkness and evil, and consequences will come upon us in this world. We as Christians still sin and make mistakes, but we do not want to live in it.

To further illuminate how we cultivate this godly fear, we turn to the ultimate example: Jesus Christ Himself, who embodied the fear of the Lord in perfect harmony with the Father's will. Isaiah 11:1-2 prophesies,

> *"There shall come forth a Rod from the stem of Jesse, And a Branch shall grow out of his roots. The Spirit of the Lord shall rest upon Him, The Spirit of wisdom and understanding, The Spirit of counsel and might, The Spirit of knowledge and of the fear of the Lord."*

Here, the Spirit of the fear of the Lord rests upon Jesus, the promised Messiah. Jesus functions and operates in the fear of God as a profound reverence that guides His every action and decision. This fear is one of the sevenfold aspects of the Spirit that anoints Him, equipping Him for His mission and demonstrating that even the Son of God walks in holy awe of the Father.

Isaiah 11:3 continues,

> *"His delight is in the fear of the Lord, And He shall not judge by the sight of His eyes, Nor decide by the hearing of His ears."*

Jesus delights in the fear of the Lord, finding joy and satisfaction in this reverential posture. He knows what to fear and what not to fear, discerning with divine wisdom rather than relying on human senses. The fear of the Lord is such a driving force in Jesus' life that He is absolutely void of any other kind of fear. He faces storms, demons, and opposition without flinching, because His heart is anchored in awe of the Father. Jesus is so fearless because of a proper fear, a godly fear, working in His heart, freeing Him from the snares of man or circumstance. This same fear empowers believers today, transforming our anxieties into bold obedience as we follow His pattern.

Hebrews 5:7 provides a poignant glimpse into how this fear manifests in Jesus' earthly ministry:

> *"Who, in the days of His flesh, when He had offered up prayers and supplications, with vehement cries and tears to Him who was able to save Him from death, and was heard because of His godly fear."*

In the Garden of Gethsemane, Jesus prays with intense emotion, submitting to the Father's will even unto death on the cross. His godly fear ensures that His pleas are heard, not out of compulsion but out of deep honor for God's sovereignty. This fear does not paralyze Him; instead, it propels Him toward perfect obedience, as Philippians 2:8 describes:

> *"And being found in appearance as a man, He humbled Himself and became obedient to the point of death, even the death of the cross."*

Jesus' life teaches us that fearing God involves humble alignment with His purposes, trusting that His ways lead to life even through suffering. He prioritizes the Father's approval over human threats, as seen when He cleanses the temple in John 2:13-17, driven by zeal for God's house without regard for the religious leaders' backlash. In Luke 2:52, Scripture notes that,

> *"Jesus increased in wisdom and stature, and in favor with God and men,"*

indicating His growth in reverential fear that fosters divine favor. As Christians, we have this example to emulate: by delighting in the fear of the Lord as Jesus does, we gain wisdom to navigate life's trials, depart from evil, and draw near to God in spirit and truth, unlocking the secrets of His covenant in our daily walk.

STANDING IN AWE OF GOD

Building on the example of Jesus, who delights in the fear of the Lord and operates in perfect reverence toward the Father, we now explore the essence of this godly fear as standing in awe of God. There is a fear of God that is a healthy, wholesome fear, one that captivates the heart and draws us nearer to Him rather than driving us away. Part of the fear of the Lord is to be awestruck by the awesomeness of God, marveling at His infinite attributes that surpass human comprehension. When you fear God, you honor His word, recognizing it as the ultimate authority and guide for life. To fear God is to honor God, while to have no fear of God is to dishonor Him, treating His majesty with indifference or contempt. The best definition of a healthy godly fear is to stand in awe of God, a profound sense of wonder that encompasses His entire being.

Awe means you are just in awe of His majesty, power, mercy and goodness. And in that awe, it leads you to repentance through the goodness of God, as His lovingkindness reveals your need for Him and stirs a desire to align with His holiness. When you see the unveiled majesty of God that affects you deeply in your heart and produces a supernatural holiness in your life, there is a departing from evil. When you see how awesome He is by revelation, it produces holiness in your life, not through forced compliance but through transformed desires. When Scripture says,

"the fear of the Lord is to depart from evil," (Proverbs 3:7)

there is a fearing of God that literally leads you to repentance. The fear of the Lord is an awesome dread of displeasing Him, not being scared of Him, but a reverent concern born of love and respect.

Consider Psalm 33:8, which declares,

> *"Let all the earth fear the Lord; Let all the inhabitants of the world stand in awe of Him!"*

This verse calls the entire creation to a posture of awe, linking fear directly to wonder at God's sovereignty over the world He formed. It echoes throughout Scripture as a reminder that true fear begins with recognizing His creative power and providential care, inspiring all people to bow in reverence. Similarly, Romans 11:33 exclaims,

> *"Oh, the depth of the riches both of the wisdom and knowledge of God! How unsearchable are His judgments And His ways past finding out!"*

Paul stands in awe of God's infinite wisdom, acknowledging that His thoughts and plans are beyond human grasp, which humbles us and draws us into deeper worship. This awe fosters a life of gratitude and obedience, as seen in Proverbs 14:27:

> *"The fear of the Lord is a fountain of life, To turn one away from the snares of death,"*

where reverence becomes a life-giving source that guards against destruction.

If you think about someone in your life whom you respect highly, there is something worthy of imitation in their life—perhaps their integrity, wisdom, or kindness—that you value and esteem highly, and you either want to emulate it or be taught it for your own life. That is the heart of respect. If you have respect for someone, a deep-seated respect, you do not want to displease them. It is not that you are afraid or scared of them, but there is a godly fear, an awesome respect, in which you do not want to let them down. That is the way it is with God. You do not want to let Him down, and it is an awesome controlling thing in your life when you learn to fear God. This fear, rooted in awe, motivates holy living not out of terror but out of adoration, evoking a response of wonder that aligns our hearts with His righteousness. In standing in awe of God, we find the freedom to live fully for Him, departing from evil and embracing the abundant life He offers through His covenants.

REPENTING

As we stand in awe of God, captivated by His majesty and goodness that inspires a wholesome fear leading us away from evil and toward holiness, this reverence naturally propels us into repentance. Repentance is a transformative change that aligns our lives with His will. The fear of the Lord supernaturally produces repentance as we'll see in David's experience of betrayal.

Psalm 55:15-19 captures David's anguish:

> *"Let death seize them; Let them go down alive into hell, For wicked-ness is in their dwellings and among them. As for me, I will call upon God, And the Lord shall save me. Evening and morning and at noon I will pray, and cry aloud, And He shall hear my voice. He has redeemed my soul in peace from the battle that was against me, For there were many against me. God will hear, and afflict them, Even He who abides from of old. Selah Because they do not change, Therefore they do not fear God."*

David experiences brokenness in this psalm, having had his closest friends betray him and literally become his enemies. He says in this chapter that had it been an enemy who treated him this way, he could have dealt with that, but it was those who were close to him that hurt him and broke his heart. He seeks God for healing and wholeness. One of the things about the fear of the Lord and fearing God with a healthy, wholesome fear is that it supernaturally produces change in our lives. When we fear God, we change. People who do not fear God will not change. When there is no change in your life, then you do not fear God, because change is supernatural and it comes out of a reverence for God. It is the goodness of God that leads you into repentance.

To repent means to change one's mind and one's direction. This shift in thinking leads to a transformation in behavior and allegiance, turning from self-reliance, or sin, toward God. To repent is to change one's ways to the ways of God. When we repent, we realize we are on a road of darkness, on a road of destruction, going the way of the world. Jesus says that the way to destruction is broad and wide, and many people go that way, but the way of eternal life is narrow and straight (Matthew 7:13-14). When we repent, we change our mind, and God will deliver us from the powers of darkness. Acts 3:19 reinforces this:

> *"Repent therefore and be converted, that your sins may be blotted out, so that times of refreshing may come from the presence of the Lord,"*

highlighting repentance as a gateway to renewal and God's refreshing presence. Proverbs 1:7 declares:

> *"The fear of the Lord is the beginning of knowledge, But fools despise wisdom and instruction."*

If you have no fear of God, then you do not have knowledge of the kingdom of God. You do not know what is right, what is wrong, or what truth is. Proverbs 1:29 adds:

"Because they hated knowledge And did not choose the fear of the Lord."

People who do not fear God hate knowledge; they hate truth, what is right, and they hate what is God. In the Old Testament, the Hebrew word for repentance, *shub*, means to turn back or return, often implying a return to God from wayward paths, as in Ezekiel 18:30-32:

> *"'Therefore I will judge you, O house of Israel, every one according to his ways,' says the Lord God. 'Repent, and turn from all your transgressions, so that iniquity will not be your ruin. Cast away from you all the transgressions which you have committed, and get yourselves a new heart and a new spirit. For why should you die, O house of Israel? For I have no pleasure in the death of one who dies,' says the Lord God. 'Therefore turn and live!'"*

This call to repentance echoes God's heart for restoration rather than destruction.

Matthew 4:17 records:

> *"From that time Jesus began to preach and to say, 'Repent, for the kingdom of heaven is at hand.'"*

The way you enter eternity is to repent. Jesus' ministry begins with this urgent call, linking repentance to the inbreaking of God's kingdom and inviting all to turn from sin to the righteousness found in Him. As 2 Corinthians 7:10 explains,

> *"For godly sorrow produces repentance to salvation, not to be regretted; but the sorrow of the world produces death."*

True repentance arises from a godly sorrow that leads to life-changing transformation, fueled by the fear of the Lord that honors His goodness and draws us into eternal fellowship.

FEAR AND DEPENDENCY

In this chapter, we have unraveled the profound truth of fearing God, contrasting the snares of fearing man and the distortions of religious fear with the liberating reverence that draws us into intimacy with Him. We examined how departing from the law's curses frees us under the New Covenant to perfect holiness through awe-inspired fear, learned practical ways to cultivate this fear through the Spirit and the Word as exemplified by Jesus, stood in awe of God's majesty that inspires departure from evil, and embraced repentance as the supernatural change born from recognizing His goodness. This godly fear unlocks the secret of the Lord, revealing His covenants as unbreakable bonds of love and faithfulness that empower us to live boldly in His purposes. As we grasp this reverence, it transforms our hearts, aligning us with His eternal promises and equipping us to navigate life's battles with confidence in His unchanging character.

Yet, true fear of God extends beyond awe and repentance into a profound dependency on Him, where we relinquish self-reliance and trust wholly in His provision and guidance. In the next chapter, we will explore this dependency, examining how it flows from covenant relationship and enables us to partner with God in ways that surpass our natural abilities, drawing from biblical examples that illustrate the joy and power of leaning on His strength rather than our own.

CHAPTER 13

DEPENDING ON GOD

L et's turn our gaze to a natural fruit of covenantal bonds: dependency on God. There's a human struggle for independence, a rebellion against God's design of dependency. But to live in covenant with God is to lean wholly on Him, to rest in His provision, and to trust His faithfulness, not as a last resort, but as a daily posture of faith. At its core, dependency on God is a condition of the heart that recognizes its need for Him, not out of weakness in the worldly sense, but out of trust in the strength of the One who has bound Himself to us. When God enters covenant with us, He doesn't offer a set of rules or promises to be admired from afar. He invites us into a partnership where we can rely on Him completely.

This chapter will explore how understanding God's covenants leads us to depend on Him, not as a last resort, but as a continual, life-giving stance. We'll see this dependency modeled in the lives of two of Israel's leaders—Hezekiah and Asa in his cautionary tale. Through these stories, we'll discover that dependency on God, rooted in covenant, is not about earning His favor but receiving it, not about despair but about assurance.

PSALM 81:8-10 – INVITATION TO DEPENDENCY

"Hear, O My people, and I will admonish you! O Israel, if you will listen to Me! There shall be no foreign god among you; Nor shall you worship any foreign god. I am the Lord your God, Who brought you out of the land of Egypt; Open your mouth wide, and I will fill it." (Psalm 81:8-10)

These words, penned by Asaph, are more than a poetic flourish, they are a covenantal summons. God speaks to Israel as *"the Lord your God,"* a title reflecting relational intimacy. He reminds them of their deliverance from Egypt, a mighty act rooted in the Abrahamic covenant, where God swore by Himself to bless Abraham's seed and bring them into a land of promise (Genesis 15:17-18). This exodus was the fulfillment of a sacred oath, a testament to God's fidelity to His word.

Here, God calls Israel to listen, to hearken to His voice alone, forsaking the false gods that tempt them to self-reliance. The climax of this call is striking: *"Open your mouth wide, and I will fill it."* Picture a nest of baby birds, frail and helpless, their oversized beaks gaping as they await their mother's provision. Inside, you see tiny creatures, small scraps of flesh crowned with oversized beaks. Their bodies are frail, their eyes barely open, their feathers yet to grow. They can't hunt, can't fly, and can't even stand. When the mother bird returns, tapping the nest's edge, those beaks spring to life, stretching wide in a chorus of chirps. They don't calculate where the food comes from or whether it's enough; they simply open their mouths, trusting she'll drop nourishment into their waiting throats. If she delays, their little heads droop, exhausted from the effort, but the moment she arrives, they revive, fully dependent on her care.

This is the picture God paints for Israel, and for us. We are that baby bird, weak in our flesh, unable to sustain ourselves apart from Him. In John 15:5, Jesus echoes this truth:

"Without Me you can do nothing."

God's not condemning us; this is by design. God created us for dependency, not independence. Refer back to Adam as a covenant head representing humanity, his fall plunging us all into frailty (Romans 5:12). Yet, through Jesus, our ultimate covenant head, we're grafted back into relationship with God (Romans 11:17). Our weakness isn't a flaw to overcome but a feature to embrace, a reminder that our life flows from Him alone.

Contrast this with the world's mantra of self-sufficiency. From childhood, we're taught to stand on our own, to carve our own path. Society lauds the self-made, the independent, those who need no one. But God's design flips this upside down. In Genesis 1:26-27, He made us in His image, not to be solitary islands but to reflect His relational nature, a trinity of interdependence. When Adam walked with God in Eden (Genesis 3:8), he depended on Him for purpose and provision. Sin fractured that reliance, birthing a prideful quest for autonomy that still haunts us today. Israel's history mirrors this: when they forgot their covenant, they turned to idols—Baal, Asherah, golden calves—seeking control apart from God. Each time, dependency on substitutes led to bondage, not freedom.

THE FOLLY OF INDEPENDENCE

This human bent toward independence is a rebellion against God's blueprint. Psalm 81:11-12 reveals the cost:

> *"But My people would not heed My voice, And Israel would have none of Me. So I gave them over to their own stubborn heart, To walk in their own counsels."*

To reject dependency on God is to court disaster. When Israel spurned Him, they didn't find liberty; they found lust, idolatry, and exile. The phrase *"gave them over"* is chilling. One of God's severest judgments is to let us have what we demand apart from Him. In 1 Samuel 8, Israel begged for a king, yearning to be like other nations rather than rely on God as their sovereign. He granted their request, but the kings, from Saul's jealousy to Solomon's excess, often led them deeper into trouble.

Today, this pattern persists. When we refuse to open our mouths wide to God, we turn to substitutes. Some lean on drugs or alcohol to numb pain, others chase materialism or sexual perversion for fulfillment. These are counterfeit dependencies, promising what only God can deliver. In Romans 1:25, Paul describes this exchange:

> *"Who exchanged the truth of God for the lie, and worshiped and served the creature rather than the Creator."*

The result? Co-dependency, an unhealthy reliance on people or things that ensnare rather than liberate. God warns in Psalm 81:9,

> *"There shall be no foreign god among you,"*

because He knows these idols can't fill us; they only hollow us out.

Yet, God's design isn't to shame our weakness but to redirect it. In 2 Corinthians 12:9, Paul hears God say,

> *"My grace is sufficient for you, for My strength is made perfect in weakness."*

Dependency on God isn't a crutch for the feeble, it's the strength of the wise. Israel's victories—think Jericho's walls tumbling (Joshua 6) or Gideon's 300 routing Midian (Judges 7)—came not from might but from reliance on Him. Our culture may scorn neediness, but Scripture celebrates it as the gateway to God's power.

HEZEKIAH'S TRUST DURING CRISIS

To see this dependency lived out, let's turn to Hezekiah who leaned on God's covenant when human strength was not enough. His story, rooted in the Davidic and Abrahamic covenants, show how reliance on God turns desperation into deliverance.

In 2 Kings 19, the Assyrian king, Sennacherib, had swept through the region, conquering city after city with ruthless efficiency and now threatens Jerusalem. His strategy was as psychological as it was military: he sent messengers with letters to each city, mocking their gods and demanding surrender:

> *"Don't trust your God—He can't save you. Look at the nations we've crushed; their gods failed them."* (paraphrased from 2 Kings 18:33-35)

Most cities crumbled under this pressure, their false gods powerless to save them. But when the messenger reached Jerusalem, Hezekiah faced a different choice.

The odds were overwhelming. Assyria's army dwarfed Judah's, and defeat seemed certain. Yet Hezekiah didn't panic or negotiate. He took the letter to the temple, spread it before the Lord, and prayed,

> *"O Lord our God, I pray, save us from his hand, that all the kingdoms of the earth may know that You are the Lord God, You alone."* (2 Kings 19:19)

This is a plea born from covenant faith. He appeals to God as *"our God,"* invoking their sacred bond.

Hezekiah's dependency shines in his actions. He didn't rely on military might or alliances, options Judah barely had anyway. Instead, he turned to the God who had bound Himself to Israel through the covenants with Abraham, Moses, and David. God's response through the prophet Isaiah reveals the basis of this deliverance:

> *"For I will defend this city, to save it For My own sake and for My servant David's sake."* (2 Kings 19:34)

Notice the reasoning. God didn't say, "I'll save you because of your righteousness, Hezekiah, or because Judah deserves it." He said it's for *"His own sake,"* His reputation as a covenant-keeping God, and for *"David's sake,"* honoring the everlasting promise made in 2 Samuel 7:16. That night, an angel struck down 185,000 Assyrian soldiers, and Sennacherib fled (2 Kings 19:35-36). Judah didn't lift a sword. Their dependency on God, anchored in covenant, brought victory. Hezekiah opened his mouth wide, humbly admitting weakness, and God filled it with deliverance.

ASA'S MISPLACED DEPENDENCY

Consider the stark contrast presented by Asa, the father of Jehoshaphat, whose actions in 2 Chronicles 16 unfold as a cautionary tale of misplaced trust. Earlier in his reign, Asa had known the power of relying on God. When a formidable army of Cushites and Libyans, vast in number with countless chariots and horsemen, marched against Judah, Asa turned to the Lord in desperation and faith. He prayed,

> *"Lord, there is no one like you to help the powerless against the mighty,"* (2 Chronicles 14:11, NIV)

and God responded with a resounding victory, delivering the enemy into Judah's hands. This moment stood as a testament to God's faithfulness to those who depend on Him.

Yet, years later, when faced with a new threat, this time from Baasha, the king of Israel, Asa's resolve faltered. Instead of seeking God as he had before, he turned to human ingenuity. He stripped silver and gold from the treasuries of the Lord's temple and sent them as a bribe to Ben-Hadad, king of Aram, persuading him to break his treaty with Israel and attack them instead. On the surface, this alliance appeared successful: Ben-Hadad's assault diverted Israel's attention, granting Judah a temporary reprieve. But this was no true victory, it was a fleeting solution born of independence rather than faith.

Enter Hanani the seer, who confronted Asa with a message both piercing and profound:

> *"Because you relied on the king of Aram and not on the Lord your God, the army of the king of Aram has escaped from your hand. Were not the Cushites and Libyans a mighty army with great numbers of chariots and horsemen? Yet when you relied on the Lord, he delivered them into your hand. For the eyes of the Lord range throughout the earth to strengthen those whose hearts are fully committed to him. You have done a foolish thing, and from now on you will be at war."* (2 Chronicles 16:7-9, NIV)

Hanani's rebuke cuts to the core: Asa's choice to lean on human aid rather than divine strength cost him more than he realized. Not only did he miss an opportunity for God to once again demonstrate His power, perhaps even subduing Aram as a threat entirely, but he also sowed the seeds of ongoing conflict. The very peace he sought through his alliance slipped through his fingers, replaced by persistent wars that plagued the remainder of his reign. Dependency on God had once been his fortress; independence proved to be his folly.

This narrative echoes loudly in the lives of many believers today. So often, the wars that rage within us, turmoil in our hearts, strife in our families, chaos in our communities, stem from a refusal or a failure to rely on the Lord. Some reject this reliance out of pride, others simply haven't been taught how to trust God fully, leaving them to battle life's challenges with their own frail resources.

The result? Anxiety festers, relationships fracture, and purpose fades, wars of the soul that mirror the external conflicts Asa invited. Yet, Scripture offers us better models. We need to emulate Jehoshaphat (his dependency on God was discussed in Chapter 9) and Hezekiah, men who understood their covenant with God and appealed to Him on that basis. When Jehoshaphat faced a coalition of enemies, he didn't scramble for alliances; he proclaimed a fast and prayed,

> *"Nor do we know what to do, but our eyes are upon You,"* (2 Chronicles 20:12)

and God fought the battle for him. Likewise, Hezekiah, confronted by the Assyrian threat, laid the enemy's taunts before God and cried,

> *"O Lord our God, I pray, save us from his hand, that all the kingdoms of the earth may know that You are the Lord God, You alone."* (2 Kings 19:19)

God answered with deliverance, proving His covenant faithfulness. These kings didn't wait for human solutions. Instead, they ran to the God who had promised to be their strength.

So why do we wait until the bottom falls out? Why do we delay until our marriages teeter on collapse, our children spiral into addiction, or our lives unravel in despair before we turn to God? Is it ignorance of His promises, or a deeper flaw within us? What is it in our character that drives us, in our pride, to be humbled by life's challenges and the bitter consequences of our actions, rather than rising each morning to live in covenant with God? Perhaps it's the shadow of the fall, an ingrained bent toward self-sufficiency, a stubborn desire to control our own destinies. Yet, life's humbling lessons reveal our limits time and again, pointing us back to the truth Asa forgot: our strength lies not in ourselves, but in the God whose eyes roam the earth, eager to uphold those who commit their hearts to Him.

Here's the good news: you can live in this reliance every day, and it's incredible what God can do in a life surrendered to Him. You don't have to wait for the impossible to cry out. Imagine beginning each day with a simple declaration: "Lord, I depend on You for my needs, my guidance, my strength." This posture transforms the mundane into the miraculous, inviting God's provision and power into every moment. Asa's wars teach us the cost of independence; Jehoshaphat and Hezekiah show us the peace of dependence. The choice is ours. Will we trust in fleeting human solutions, or will we lean on the God who promises to be our fortress?

THE STRUGGLE TO DEPEND

Despite these examples, dependency doesn't come easily. Our human nature resists it, conditioned by a world that prizes self-sufficiency. We want to earn God's favor, to deserve His blessings, as if our performance could add to His covenant. This pride, subtle or overt, whispers that dependency is weakness, not strength. Yet Scripture counters this:

"When I am weak, then I am strong," (2 Corinthians 12:10)

Paul writes, because God's power shines in our reliance on Him.

Another barrier is our tendency to depend on God only in crisis. Hezekiah and Jehoshaphat turned to Him when armies loomed, but what about the quiet days? Too often, we wait until things have already crashed down—marriages collapse, finances crumble, health fails—before we cry out. Why? Our pride resists daily humility, preferring control until control slips away. But God invites us to a lifestyle of dependency, but not as a last resort. Psalm 81:10 isn't for emergencies alone; it's a daily call to trust Him for,

"our daily bread," (Matthew 6:11)

and every need.

LIVING DEPENDENCY TODAY

So, what does this mean for us under the New Covenant? Through Jesus, our covenant head, we're invited to open our mouths wide daily. Here's how this unfolds practically.

First, we recognize it's about receiving, not earning. Mephibosheth had to accept David's kindness; we must accept God's through Christ. Ephesians 2:8-9 reminds us,

> *"By grace you have been saved through faith, and that not of yourselves; it is the gift of God, not of works, lest anyone should boast."*

Dependency starts with faith in what's already done.

Second, we confront unworthiness. Like Mephibosheth, we may feel like *"dead dogs,"* but God sees us through covenant eyes. Romans 8:1 declares,

> *"There is therefore now no condemnation to those who are in Christ Jesus."*

We don't warm up to God; He's already warm to us.

Third, we practice gratitude. Psalm 107:8 says,

"Oh that men would give thanks to the Lord for His goodness, and for His wonderful works to the children of men!"

Thanking God daily for His lovingkindness reinforces our trust.

Finally, we choose trust in every moment. Whether facing giants or mundane challenges, we echo Jehoshaphat:

"We do not know what to do, but our eyes are upon you." (2 Chronicles 20:12)

This isn't blind faith; it's faith in a God who's proven Himself through covenant, from Abraham's stars to Christ's cross.

Dependency on God is the heartbeat of covenant life. It's not a crutch for the weak but a crown for the wise who know their strength lies in Him. Hezekiah saw armies fall and Jehoshaphat watched enemies scatter all because they leaned on a God who cannot break His word. As we stand under the New Covenant, we're invited to open our mouths wide daily like a baby bird, trusting Jesus, our covenant head, to fill them. This dependency isn't bondage; it's freedom, not shame, but glory. For in His covenant, we find a God who says, "I am yours, depend on Me, and I will never let you go."

CHAPTER 14

FAITH IN GOD

Your very faith is established in covenant, rooted in the unbreakable promises of God that span from creation to the cross. When you receive a word from God, faith arises by hearing and continually engaging with that word, as Romans 10:17 declares:

"So then faith comes by hearing, and hearing by the word of God."

Yet, standing firm on any divine promise requires it to be grounded in covenant where we need to trust in His faithfulness. This dependency on God is a covenantal reality that invites us to lean wholly on His word, transforming uncertainty into unshakeable confidence. True faith demands we anchor ourselves in these divine pacts, where God's commitments become the bedrock of our spiritual lives.

Colossians 2:6-7 (NIV) captures this essence beautifully:

"So then, just as you received Christ Jesus as Lord, continue to live your lives in him, rooted and built up in him, strengthened in the faith as you were taught, and overflowing with thankfulness."

This verse emphasizes living covenantally in Christ, where our faith is established and strengthened like roots in fertile soil, providing a firm foundation through His New Covenant. Paul wrote these words to a young church in Colossae, facing pressures from false teachings that mixed philosophy, legalism, and mysticism, ideas suggesting that simple faith in Christ wasn't enough. Instead, Paul urges believers to persist in the gospel they first received, growing deeper in Christ rather than chasing additions or distractions. The imagery of being *"rooted"* speaks to hidden, nourishing growth through Scripture, prayer, and obedience, while *"built up"* evokes a structure rising steadily under God's guidance.

We don't earn God's provision; we just have to trust Him for it. When we lack faith, we end up with our own messes—like Abraham's attempt to "help" God by fathering Ishmael, which birthed generations of conflict. But when we lean into Him, He meets us with abundance, as seen in the covenants that promise inheritance of the world, forgiveness apart from works, and righteousness by faith alone (Romans 4). Abraham wasn't instantly convinced; his faith grew over years of hearing God's promises, stumbling, and being met where he was. Similarly, God works with us patiently, urging us to open wider to His possibilities. So, what's it gonna be—our way, with its limitations and failures, or His, overflowing with covenantal blessings?

THE STRAIGHT AND NARROW WAY

This brings us to a passage often misunderstood in Matthew 7:13-14, where Jesus says:

> *"Enter by the narrow gate; for wide is the gate and broad is the way that leads to destruction, and there are many who go in by it. Because narrow is the gate and difficult is the way which leads to life, and there are few who find it."*

Too often, we've twisted this into a picture of a harsh, restrictive God, making salvation difficult, as if He's reluctant to let us in. But that's not what Jesus means. The narrow gate isn't about hardship; it's about exclusivity. There is only one way to life, and that way is Him.

Jesus is the narrow gate, the seed of Abraham, the Son of David, the mediator of the New Covenant. His death on the cross initiated the covenant we enter by faith, and there's no other path to God. The wide gate represents the myriad ways people seek salvation such as good works, religion, or self-righteousness which all lead to destruction because they bypass the one true door. The narrowness isn't a barrier to keep people out; it's a focus on the singular truth of Christ. As John 14:6 declares,

> *"I am the way, the truth, and the life. No one comes to the Father except through Me."*

Far from wanting to exclude us, God sent Jesus to save the whole world. We are assured in 2 Peter 3:9,

> *"The Lord is not willing that any should perish but that all should come to repentance."*

He's not trying to keep people out; He's inviting everyone in through the one gate that stands open to all who believe. Once we enter, we step into the kingdom of God, secure in His covenant, and our faith finds its footing in the certainty of His provision.

OVERVIEW OF MAJOR COVENANTS

To grasp how faith is established in covenant, we must survey the major covenants God made, each a stepping stone in His redemptive plan. Most of these covenants remain active, shaping our relationship with Him today, save for one superseded by the New Covenant. Let's briefly trace these back, focusing on their enduring relevance without delving into the depths to be explored in books of their own.

The Covenant with Creation anchors the natural order: day and night, seed-time and harvest, cold and heat (Genesis 8:22). God bound Himself to sustain the world, a universal promise that holds to this day. Every sunrise testifies to His faithfulness, a covenant that encompasses all humanity, the animal kingdom, and the earth itself. Through it, He gave us dominion, a stewardship still ours despite the fall.

The Covenant with Adam set terms of obedience in Eden (Genesis 2:15-17). Adam and Eve's choice to eat from the Tree of Knowledge of Good and Evil broke that bond, and we still bear the consequences, judgment follows disobedience. We're still "eating" from that tree whenever we choose our way over God's, facing the consequences. Yet, this covenant's echo reminds us of our need for a Redeemer, pointing forward to the One who would restore what was lost.

The Covenant with Noah is a pledge of preservation (Genesis 9:12-17). After the flood, God vowed never again to destroy the earth with water, sealing it with the rainbow, a sign we see today. This covenant applies to all humanity, and its sign remains visible in the sky, reminding us of God's mercy and His ongoing relationship with us. It bolsters our faith by showing He preserves us despite our failings.

Then comes the Covenant with Abraham in Genesis 12:1-3 and 15:18, where God promised to make him a great nation, bless him, and bless all families of the earth through him. This covenant endures today, not limited to Abraham's physical descendants but extended to all who believe in Jesus, the seed of Abraham (Galatians 3:29). Through faith, we're spiritual heirs to these blessings, righteous-ness, inheritance, and a relationship with God. Its eternal scope assures us that God's promises are for us now, strengthening our trust in His plan.

The Covenant of the Law with Moses, given at Sinai in Exodus 19:5-6, includ-ed laws and rituals specific to Israel. It set them apart as God's people but also revealed humanity's inability to earn righteousness, pointing to a better covenant. While its ceremonial aspects are no longer binding for Christians (superseded by the New Covenant) its moral principles echo through Christ's teachings, guiding us still, reminding us of God's holiness and our need for grace.

The Covenant with David (2 Samuel 7:12-16) assures an everlasting dynasty, fulfilled in Jesus, the King of kings. This covenant points to a kingdom of peace and justice, begun at His first coming and to be fully realized at His return. It remains a living promise for believers today.

Finally, the New Covenant, prophesied in Jeremiah 31:31-34 and established through Jesus, is what we live under today. It overrules the Mosaic rituals, offering forgiveness and a restored relationship with God to all who believe, not just Israel's descendants. Sealed with Christ's blood, it promises the Holy Spirit, eternal life, and intimacy with God. We have no excuses; everything we need is available in this covenant, making the world our limit when we stand on it.

These covenants—Creation, Adamic, Noahic, Abrahamic, Davidic, and the New Covenant—apply to us today, except for Moses' law, which the New Covenant fulfills. The covenants of Creation, Adamic, and Noahic are universal and apply to everyone whether they are followers of Christ or not. The Abrahamic, Davidic, and the New Covenant through Jesus amplify our inheritance—through faith, the world is ours to impact. Together, they reveal a God who keeps His word, building our faith on His unchanging character.

ROMANS 4:5-9 – JUSTIFICATION BY FAITH

The Abrahamic Covenant is a cornerstone of biblical theology, revealing how faith, rather than works, establishes our relationship with God. In Romans 4, the Apostle Paul meticulously unpacks this covenant, using Abraham's life as a lens to illustrate the nature of righteousness, the role of covenant signs, and the expansive scope of God's promises. Let's explore in detail the Old Testament covenant with Abraham and its fulfillment in the New Testament through Jesus Christ, showing that faith is the thread that binds believers across time and nations into God's redemptive plan.

Paul begins with a radical declaration about how we are made right with God:

"But to him who does not work but believes on Him who justifies the ungodly, his faith is accounted for righteousness." (Romans 4:5)

This statement flips the script on any system that ties righteousness to human effort. Paul isn't suggesting that good behavior is irrelevant, but he's emphatic that it's not the basis for our standing with God. Instead, it's faith, trust in God's promise, that makes us righteous.

To drive this home, Paul brings in David, quoting Psalm 32:

"Just as David also describes the blessedness of the man to whom God imputes righteousness apart from works: 'Blessed are those whose lawless deeds are forgiven, and whose sins are covered; blessed is the man to whom the Lord shall not impute sin.'" (Romans 4:6-8)

David, a key figure in the Davidic Covenant, rejoices in God's mercy, not in his own merit. His words highlight forgiveness as the heart of this blessedness. Our sins aren't just overlooked; they're covered, and God doesn't hold them against us. This is the essence of justification: God declares us righteous because we trust Him, not because we've earned it.

Paul then asks,

"Does this blessedness then come upon the circumcised only, or upon the uncircumcised also? For we say that faith was accounted to Abraham for righteousness." (Romans 4:9)

Here, he's setting the stage to show that this principle isn't limited to one group. Abraham's faith was counted as righteousness, and Paul will soon clarify when and how that happened. But the connection to David is profound: the Davidic Covenant pointed forward to the Messiah, Jesus Christ, who hadn't

yet come in David's time. Yet, David's joy in forgiveness anticipates the ultimate forgiveness we receive through Christ. Abraham's faith looked forward
to the same reality, both covenants converge on the truth that righteousness
comes through faith in God's promises, not through our conduct.

This is transformative for us today. Our sins are forgiven, and we're made
right with God because we trust in the covenants God established, covenants
that find their ultimate expression in Jesus, who bore our sins and secured
our righteousness.

ROMANS 4:10 – THE TIMING OF RIGHTEOUSNESS

Paul digs deeper with a pivotal question:

> *"How then was it accounted? While he was circumcised, or un-*
> *circumcised? Not while circumcised, but while uncircumcised."*
> (Romans 4:10)

This isn't a trivial detail, it's a theological bombshell. To understand why,
we need to look back at Abraham's story in Genesis. In Genesis 15:6, we're
told,

> *"He believed in the Lord, and He accounted it to him for right-*
> *eousness."*

This moment of faith happens before God institutes circumcision in Genesis 17. Abraham was made right with God before he received the covenant
cutting of circumcision.

Why does this matter? Because it proves that circumcision didn't make Abraham righteous. Paul will elaborate in the next verse, but the point here is clear:
righteousness came through faith, not through the ritual. Circumcision was a
sign and a seal of the righteousness Abraham already had. It's like a signature on

a contract that's already been agreed upon, it confirms the deal, but it doesn't create it.

This timing ties back to Romans 4:9, where Paul links Abraham's justification to the forgiveness David celebrated. David gloried in God's mercy and grace, and Abraham's story shows that this mercy precedes any outward act. When Romans was written, the full Bible as we know it didn't exist, but Paul had the Torah and the Psalms to draw from. Today, we have the complete Scriptures, and we see the same truth: Abraham was justified by faith in Genesis, long before circumcision sealed it.

THE PARALLEL TO WATER BAPTISM

This principle carries over into the New Testament with striking clarity. The closest parallel we have to circumcision under the new covenant is water baptism. Just as circumcision didn't make Abraham right with God, water baptism doesn't save us. It's a seal of the covenant we've already entered by faith, not the means of entering it.

Scripture teaches that we're made right by faith in the cross: Jesus' sacrifice, His shed blood, and His resurrection.

> *"For by grace you have been saved through faith, and that not of yourselves; it is the gift of God, not of works, lest anyone should boast."*
> (Ephesians 2:8-9)

Baptism follows as an act of obedience and a public declaration of that faith. Peter calls it,

> *"not the removal of the filth of the flesh, but the answer of a good conscience toward God."* (1 Peter 3:21)

It's a response to salvation, not the cause of it.

Yet, this is a point of confusion for many, just as it was in Paul's day. The Jews began to see circumcision as the source of their righteousness, not as a sign pointing to faith in God's promise. Similarly, some today think baptism itself saves, missing the deeper reality it represents. Paul's argument in Romans 4 corrects this error: righteousness comes through faith, and the covenant sign, whether circumcision or baptism, affirms what's already true by faith.

ROMANS 4:11-12 – UNIVERSALITY OF THE COVENANT

Paul builds on this foundation:

> *"And he received the sign of circumcision, a seal of the righteousness of the faith which he had while still uncircumcised, that he might be the father of all those who believe, though they are uncircumcised, that righteousness might be imputed to them also, and the father of circumcision to those who not only are of the circumcision, but who also walk in the steps of the faith which our father Abraham had while still uncircumcised."* (Romans 4:11-12)

Here's the game-changer: Abraham's faith makes him the father of all believers, not just the circumcised.

This universality is breathtaking. Righteousness isn't restricted to those who bear the physical sign of the covenant; it's imputed to everyone who shares Abraham's faith. Jews who follow in his footsteps of faith are his children, but so are Gentiles who believe without ever being circumcised. This fulfills God's promise in Genesis 12:3:

> *"In you all the families of the earth shall be blessed."*

Through faith, people from every nation are grafted into the Abrahamic Covenant, a truth Paul later explores in Romans 11:17.

For us, this means the covenant isn't an exclusive club. It's open to anyone who trusts in God's promises, as Abraham did. Our faith in Christ connects us to this ancient covenant, making us heirs of the same blessings Abraham received.

ROMANS 4:13 – SCOPE OF THE PROMISE

Paul then expands the promise's horizon:

> *"For the promise that he would be the heir of the world was not to Abraham or to his seed through the law, but through the righteousness of faith."* (Romans 4:13)

Paul wasn't just talking about a small plot of land in Canaan, it's about the world. Abraham wasn't fixated on boundaries in the Middle East; he saw something bigger. The physical land was a type and shadow, a down payment on a grander inheritance.

Hebrews 11:10 tells us Abraham,

> *"waited for the city which has foundations, whose builder and maker is God."*

He knew God's promise transcended dirt and borders, it encompassed the entire earth. This is why Jesus, in Matthew 5:5, declares,

> *"Blessed are the meek, for they shall inherit the earth."*

The meek, those who trust God like Abraham, will inherit not just a region, but the world. This is the kingdom of God breaking into history, where God's reign extends over all creation.

The Abrahamic Covenant, then, isn't a footnote in Israel's story; it's a cosmic promise. Through faith, Abraham and his seed, ultimately Christ and all who are in Him (Galatians 3:16, 29), become heirs of a renewed earth. This ties the covenant to the ultimate restoration of all things, a hope we still cling to today.

ROMANS 4:19-22 – ABRAHAM'S FAITH JOURNEY

Finally, Paul reflects on Abraham's faith:

> *"And not being weak in faith, he did not consider his own body, already dead (since he was about a hundred years old), and the deadness of Sarah's womb. He did not waver at the promise of God through unbelief, but was strengthened in faith, giving glory to God, and being fully convinced that what He had promised He was also able to perform. And therefore 'it was accounted to him for righteousness.'"* (Romans 4:19-22)

This paints Abraham as a titan of faith, but his journey wasn't that simple. Abraham didn't wake up with unshakable trust. When God promised him a son in Genesis 15, he was already old, and Sarah was barren. Doubt crept in, and he tried to "help" God by fathering Ishmael through Hagar (Genesis 16). That decision birthed a headache, a problem that rippled through generations, as Ishmael's line clashed with Isaac's. Abraham wasn't fully persuaded at first; he stumbled, just as we do.

But faith isn't static. Over time, through God's repeated assurances, like the covenant ceremony in Genesis 15 and the reaffirmation in Genesis 17, Abraham grew. By Genesis 21, when Isaac was born, he was *"fully convinced"* that God could do the impossible. His faith was strengthened through hearing God's word and seeing His faithfulness, giving glory to God even when logic said it couldn't happen.

This is encouraging for us. Faith isn't an overnight miracle; it's a process. We may try to "help" God with our own Ishmaels, our attempts to fix what He's promised to handle. But God doesn't abandon us there. He keeps speaking, keeps proving Himself, until we too can trust Him fully. Abraham's righteousness wasn't a reward for perfection; it was credited because he believed, even imperfectly at first.

THE SECRET REVEALED

As we reflect on the journey of faith established in God's covenant, it becomes clear that this is not a path of instant perfection but one of continual growth and deepening trust. Aren't you glad that God meets us where we are? He doesn't demand that we have it all figured out from the start. Instead, He works with us as much as we'll allow Him, gently coaxing us to trust Him more, to lean into His promises, and to open ourselves wider to His blessings. Like a patient parent, God is always encouraging us: "You can, you can, you can—just open that beak a little wider."

Too often, we think we've arrived, that we've opened ourselves as much as possible, only to realize our beak is only half open. There's more, always more, that God wants to pour into our lives. We may believe for a season, get excited about His promises, and then stumble, crash, and burn in moments of weakness. In those times, doubt creeps in, and we wonder if God will still bless us. But God looks at us, not with disappointment, but with love. He sees a little bird, frail in flesh, yet He doesn't ask for our flesh to be stronger. He simply says, "Open your mouth wider." He's not waiting for us to perfect ourselves; He's inviting us to receive more of what He's already prepared.

This journey of faith isn't about overnight transformation. You don't get fully persuaded about the things of God in a single moment. Abraham didn't become fully convinced in a day, and neither will we. There will be times when we try to help God along, producing our own Ishmaels—our well-intentioned but misguided efforts. Yet, even in those missteps, God remains faithful. He keeps speaking, keeps revealing His heart, and keeps urging us to trust Him more fully. His desire is not to shame us for our doubts but to draw us into deeper reliance on His covenant promises.

And what promises they are! God declares that He'll do more for you than you ever dreamed. He'll do more for you than you can believe Him for right now. He is able to do,

> *"exceeding abundantly above all that we ask or think, according to the power that works in us."* (Ephesians 3:20)

To unlock this secret, remember that it is all about our relationship with God. It begins with fearing Him with reverential awe, approaching Him not in dread but in worshipful honor of His majesty and goodness. This fear draws us near, opening our hearts to His presence and aligning our lives with His holiness. From there, we learn to depend on Him for everything, surrendering our self-reliance and trusting that He provides our every need, from daily sustenance to eternal hope. This dependence fosters intimacy, as we lean on His strength rather than our own, allowing His power to work through our weaknesses. And as we grow in this relationship, we must increase our faith, stepping beyond doubt into bold assurance in His promises. Faith grows through hearing His Word, meditating on His covenants, and acting on His truths, even when circumstances challenge us. Like Abraham, who grew strong in faith by giving glory to God despite impossible odds, we too can build our faith by recalling His past faithfulness and expecting His future provision. In this relational journey, marked by awe, dependence, and growing faith, God reveals His covenant secrets, transforming us from hesitant believers into confident partners in His eternal plan.

This isn't a distant hope; it's a present reality for those who act in faith and receive the covenant already provided. As we open wider, as we trust Him more, the secret of the Lord, His covenant, unfolds before us, revealing the depths of His love, His faithfulness, and His unbreakable commitment to us.

So, keep opening wider. Let your faith be stretched, not by striving, but by receiving. For in this covenant, you are not alone, and you are not limited by your own strength. God is with you, working in you, and He has more, always more, for those who fear and depend on Him.

www.ingramcontent.com/pod-product-compliance
Lightning Source LLC
Chambersburg PA
CBHW020405150626
46554CB00012B/293